PRAISE FOR *INVENTING AMERICA*
(Companion book for the PBS series)

"Insightful...entertaining...a reminder of how much we owe our forefathers."
–Richard Beeman, author *of Our Lives, Our Fortune & Our Sacred Honor: The Forging of American Independence*

"Milton Nieuwsma's dream of finding a creative, compelling way to retell the story of our nation's start is vividly on display in these dialogues. Each episode is filled with personality and insight—as if the writer himself befriended the founders and brought them together. *Inventing America* is a terrific way to introduce our nation's founders to a new generation of readers.
–Gleaves Whitney, Director, Hauenstein Center for Presidential Studies

"This brilliant and entertaining book brings our founders to life as unique individuals, revealing all their genius, their bravery, their occasional arrogance and lechery, which make them truly Americans. We recognize them individually here as the best of us, each with imperfections that render them endearingly real. The history they made together has never been more accessibly or humanely told."
–Richard P. Hiskes, Professor Emeritus, Political Science and Human Rights, University of Connecticut

"Clear, concise, relevant, *Inventing America* is an invaluable resource for students of America history. It shows how our forefathers confronted the challenge every generation of Americans faces: 'What kind of government shall we have?' Best of all, it provides us with insight into how to define American political life for our time."

–John M. Mulder, historian/theologian; award-winning author of *Woodrow Wilson: The Years of Preparation*

"At this moment in our nation's history, we need to take every opportunity to revisit the minds of the founders. *Inventing America* is a wonderful way to do that."
–Marc Baer, Professor Emeritus of History, Hope College, Holland, Mich.

PRAISE FOR *KINDERLAGER*
(Later published as *Surviving Auschwitz*)

"These stories are heartbreaking, and yet, some moments miraculously radiate hope."
—Elie Wiesel, Nobel Laureate

"Oral history becomes an art form as (Nieuwsma) records the memories of three women who survived *Kinderlager*, the children's camp at Auschwitz-Birkenau.... A compelling one-sitting read."
—*Foreword*

"Heartrending...An important piece of Holocaust literature."
—*Chicago Tribune*

"A remarkable gift of insight to the Holocaust years and its implications for all of us."
—*The Horn Book*

"The stories are well and simply told."
—*VOYA*

"These accounts combine the immediacy of the child's experience with the sophistication of adult hindsight. Like Anita Lovel in *No Pretty Pictures*, these women refuse to play celebrity or victim."
—*Booklist*

"Nieuwsma has done an impressive job of capturing the children's voices."
—*Publisher's Weekly*

"A phenomenal experience in reading."
—*Jewish World News*

"Powerfully written and heart-wrenching."
—*The Reading Corner*

"An extraordinary oral history."
—*Cooperative Children's Book Center*

MIRACLE ON CHESTNUT STREET

The Untold Story
of Thomas Jefferson
and the
Declaration of Independence

MIRACLE ON CHESTNUT STREET

The Untold Story of Thomas Jefferson and the Declaration of Independence

MILTON J. NIEUWSMA

FOREWORD BY BILL BARKER

iBooks for Young Readers
New York

iBooks for Young Readers
Manhanset House
Dering Harbor, New York 11965-0342
bricktower@aol.com
www.BrickTowerPress.com

iBooks for Young Readers colophon is a trademark of J. Boylston & Company, Publishers

Library of Congress Cataloging-in-Publication Data
Miracle of Chestnut Street: The Untold Story of Thomas Jefferson and the Declaration of Independence
Nieuwsma, Milton J.

p. cm.
1. YOUNG ADULT NONFICTION / Biography & Autobiography / Presidents & First Families (US)
2. YOUNG ADULT NONFICTION / Biography & Autobiography / Historical
3. YOUNG ADULT NONFICTION / History / United States / Colonial & Revolutionary Periods
I. Title
Includes source notes

Copyright © 2021 by Milton J. Nieuwsma
ISBN: 978–1–899694–94–5, trade paper
ISBN: 978–1–899694-95-2, hardcover
First Elecronic Edition 2021
Book Design/Typeset by Mike Slizewski

To my grandchildren—Bud, Kyran, Nils, Elan, Ashtan,
Graham, and Greta—
in the hope that Jefferson's legacy
endures to their generation
and beyond

*"Proclaim liberty throughout all the land
unto all the inhabitants thereof."*

Lev. 25, v. 10

Inscription on the Liberty Bell,
Independence Hall, Philadelphia

TABLE OF CONTENTS

TABLE OF CONTENTS (Cont.)

FOREWORD

By Bill Barker

Nearly a half century after the Declaration of Independence, a fellow Virginian asked Thomas Jefferson why he wrote the document. Jefferson, in the twilight of his life, replied: "It was intended to be an expression of the American mind and to give to that expression the proper tone and spirit called for by the occasion."

The inquisitor was a gentleman named Henry Lee, of the famous Lee family of Virginia. His cousin, Richard Henry Lee, had introduced the resolution for independence in the Continental Congress. His father, Henry "Light Horse Harry" Lee, had been a cavalry commander in the Continental Army. His half-brother, Robert E. Lee, would one day lead the Confederate armies in the Civil War

Jefferson's reply, penned a year before he died, was one of the last letters he wrote. And Lee had no inkling himself that he would shed his mortal coil in little more than ten years.

The two gentlemen had more in common than their Virginia roots. In their last years, both would fall deeply in debt. Their personal lives would be tarnished by scandal. Their families would have to sell their beloved homes: the Jeffersons their Monticello; the Lees their ancestral home, Stratford Hall. Jefferson would repose through eternity on his beloved "Little Mountain" while Lee, who wound up in Paris, would spend eternity in an unmarked grave on Montmarte.

Neither could foretell their futures, but both shared a common past which included the creation of a nation—*Novus Ordo Seclorum*, a new world order founded upon a radical idea of self-government as an inherent right of mankind.

i

Milton Nieuwsma, at the beginning of his engaging book, *Miracle on Chestnut Street,* sets the scene for this shared experience. Acting as a novelist, playwright and Jefferson's Boswell, he weaves "in-the-moment" dialogue and circumstances to fill in the blanks of a remarkable sixteen months of Jefferson's early life. As a result, we the readers are ever-present in conversations with Patrick Henry, Benjamin Franklin, George Washington, John Adams and John Hancock, along with Virginia tavern-keeper Mrs. Younghusband. We become participants in this history and begin to wonder ourselves where the next scene will lead us and what the morrow will bring that could change or stay the course.

This is first-person history on the written page. But as contemporary readers we have a distinct advantage: we already know what has occurred. The profound lesson we learn as imaginary participants and eye-witnesses to these moments in history is that Jefferson and his contemporaries knew no more of what would happen the next day or next month or next year any more than we know now what will happen tomorrow or the next day, let alone two centuries from now.

So, what will future generations say of us in the 23rd century? What should we know or do now that will better their lives? To understand where we're going is to remember where we have been. We are continually molded by the past. Nieuwsma's narrative in *Miracle on Chestnut Street* is supported by historical facts known to us today. And while Jefferson may have had no idea how the time between the spring of 1775 and the summer of 1776 would transpire, he had an extraordinary grasp of history and an intuitive sense of the future.

In the same letter to Henry Lee on May 8, 1825, Jefferson wrote that the object of his declaration was "not to find out new principles or new arguments never before thought of, not merely to say things which had never been said before, but to place before mankind the common sense of the subject in terms so plain and firm as to command their assent."

Miracle on Chestnut Street brings us closer to connecting with "the common sense of the subject." We see ourselves more clearly as actors upon the luminous stage of the American story. In 1825, neither Thomas Jefferson nor Henry Lee had any idea what would befall their country thirty-five years later. The American experiment was still new. It took Abraham Lincoln to remind us where we had been only four score and seven years before. His words at Gettysburg reminded us of our faults as a nation, yet were no less "intended to be an expression of the American mind." *Miracle on Chestnut Street* reminds us the creation of our nation was indeed—and still is—a miracle.

Bill Barker is the world's premiere interpreter of Thomas Jefferson. For twenty-six years he portrayed the founding father at Colonial Williamsburg. Since 2019 he has portrayed Jefferson-in-residence at Monticello, Jefferson's Virginia home. He has also portrayed Jefferson at Independence Hall in Philadelphia, the White House, and the Palace of Versailles.

AUTHOR'S NOTE

This book is a fictionalized account of actual events— history told as a story. While liberties are taken with the narrative and spoken word, all the people, places and events are real.

—*MJN*

PROLOGUE

Philadelphia – July 4, 1776

"Pd. for 7 pr. women's gloves / 27."
—Thomas Jefferson's account book entry for July 4, 1776

At nine o'clock on Thursday morning, July 4, 1776, Tom Jefferson looked out his second story window in Philadelphia, noted that his thermometer registered 72¼ degrees, and set out for the Pennsylvania State House a few blocks away.

No one—least of all Virginia's thirty-three-year-old delegate to the Continental Congress—knew this was going to be the most important day of his life. He stopped to browse at an open-air shop on Market Street, picked out seven pairs of women's gloves, and paid the shopkeeper twenty-seven shillings, noting the price in his pocket account book.

Tom's thoughts were more on home—specifically his wife, Martha—than on politics that morning. And had he any say in the matter, he would have chosen to be home at her bedside, not in Philadelphia to be midwife at a nation's birth.

He had plenty of excuses to stay home. For one thing this was his third stint in the Congress in thirteen months. The trip alone was an ordeal; the three hundred miles from Monticello, his home in Virginia, to Philadelphia had taken seven days by horse and carriage. For another he had arrived there by default, having been chosen as an afterthought to fill in for a distant cousin. Still another was that his wife, grieving the recent death of an infant daughter, was in fragile health herself, and he was reluctant to leave her alone.

But the main reason was he didn't feel up to the job. How much could he contribute to the deliberations in Philadelphia? He had no gift for public speaking, the thing most needed in that assembly. He was more comfortable at his writing desk composing his thoughts in solitude than in the give-and-take of public debate. Moreover, his stint in the Virginia House of Burgesses where he served as a representative from his home county convinced him that he had no stomach for politics.

Yet here he was in Philadelphia about to be the leading player in the most important political drama to unfold in America. In its significance it would surpass the Pilgrims' arrival at Plymouth Rock. In succeeding centuries it would surpass such defining events as the Civil War, the Great Depression, Pearl Harbor, man's walk on the moon, even the 9/11 attack, because what happened that day would symbolize to the world more than any other event what America stands for as a nation.

And so, with an irony that seems to be history's favorite sport, young Tom Jefferson, an unknown burgess from Virginia, entered the world stage through the back door. His journey started sixteen months before with his arrival, on horseback, at Mrs. Younghusband's Tavern in Richmond Town, on the edge of the Virginia Piedmont.

CHAPTER ONE

Richmond – March 20, 1775

"Pd. for punch at Mrs. Younghusband's 1/."
—Thomas Jefferson's account book entry for March 20, 1775

It was late in the afternoon when the first of the seven hills came into view. When he reached the fork off the main-traveled road the young man reined his horse to the right and rode parallel to the river. One by one the other hills came into view, all but two draped in cedar. History doesn't record what thoughts were going through his head at that moment, but as he followed the path along the James and looked up at the seven hills of Richmond, he might have imagined Aeneas looking up at the seven hills of Rome as he approached along the Tiber. It would be a fateful trip for both.

A half mile to the east from where the young man approached the town stood the higher of the two inhabited hills, Shockoe, where James Gunn's big yellow house dominated the other buildings around it. A mile beyond that stood Richmond Hill, the smaller but more inhabited of the two, which gave the town its name. Just below the ridge stood St. John's Church. Drawing closer, he caught a glimpse of the white bell tower before it sank below the rooftops.

When he reached Mrs. Younghusband's tavern at the foot of the hill, the young man tied up his horse and went inside. A few minutes later a short, heavy-set woman with a maze of wrinkles on her face placed a bowl of punch on the table. She gazed at her customer—tall, thin, rusty-haired with luminous blue-gray eyes and a fair complexion made ruddy by daily exposure to the sun. In his blue velvet coat and white knee breeches he looked every inch like a young Virginia aristocrat.

"I'm told, madam, that you serve the best arrack punch west of the Raleigh," he said cheerfully.

Mrs. Younghusband's spacious smile revealed two missing teeth. "What's good in Williamsburg is just as good here," she countered.

Presently another man came in, a copy of the *Virginia Gazette* in hand, and joined the young man at his table. Respectfully, Tom Jefferson stood up to greet him. A man of enormous bulk, Peyton Randolph had a great stomach and a massive red face that seldom smiled or frowned. The fifty-mile trip from Williamsburg had been an ordeal for him. When he spoke he sounded like an expiring balloon.

"At least we're out of Dunmore's reach here," he said, filling his cup. "I defy him to dissolve now."

It was precisely that action by Lord Dunmore, the royal governor of Virginia who served at the pleasure of His Majesty King George III, which had sent the duly-elected burgesses back home from Williamsburg, the capital, the previous spring. Five months before that, in December 1773, a bunch of rabble-rousers in Boston, protesting the British tax on tea, had boarded three merchant ships from the East India Company and dumped three hundred and forty-two chests of tea into the harbor. Parliament retaliated by closing the Port of Boston.

Sympathizing with their sister colony to the north, the Virginia burgesses proclaimed a day of fasting and prayer. That was too much for the hot-headed Dunmore who immediately dissolved them. Before going home, however, they had met surreptitiously at the Raleigh Tavern and passed some resolutions declaring that an attack on one colony was an attack on all and must be uniformly opposed. A few months later they met again to elect delegates to that other surreptitious body, a General Congress, about to convene in Philadelphia.

Delegates from twelve of the British American colonies met that fall at Carpenter's Hall. As the speaker of

Virginia's House of Burgesses, Peyton Randolph had not only led his colony's delegation to that assembly but had been chosen to preside. At issue was whether Parliament had the authority to tax the colonies without their consent.

Tom, whose mother was Randolph's cousin, was proud of the honor given his family, but he had no regrets about missing out on the Congress. He had no desire to make the three-hundred-mile trip over dirt roads and bridgeless rivers. Besides, at thirty-one he was still a relative newcomer to Virginia politics and how much use would he be? Mostly he dreaded any absence of more than a few days from his wife and two young daughters.

Even now it seemed a blessing that he had missed the convention in Williamsburg, even though he had taken it upon himself to draft some resolutions for the Virginia delegates to take to Philadelphia. He had set out on horseback from home with the paper tucked in his traveling bag when he got sick—with dysentery no less—and had to turn back. From his bed he wrote out two copies by hand and sent one by courier to Peyton Randolph and one to Patrick Henry, a burgess from neighboring Hanover County. He hadn't heard from either since.

Randolph finished his punch. He pulled a pamphlet from his curled-up newspaper and handed it to Tom. "Here's your copy," he said.

Tom reached for the pamphlet. When he looked at the title—*A Summary View of the Rights of British America*—and read the first paragraph, he recognized the writing as his.

"I didn't intend this to be published, sir," he said, his voice registering more surprise than annoyance.

Randolph brushed it off. "No reason to fret. I wanted everyone at the convention to read it."

"So, what happened?"

"It died on the table."

Tom waited for him to continue.

"The younger ones liked it. But the older ones preferred tamer sentiments."

"Tamer sentiments?"

"Yes, tamer sentiments. They said your ideas were too radical. The resolutions that passed called for the same rights and privileges as our brothers and sisters in Great Britain. No more, no less."

Tom leafed through the pamphlet, twenty-three pages long, setting forth the proposition that the American colonies were subject to no laws but those of their own making. It was the first time he had seen any writing of his in print:

Our emigration from England to this country gave her no more rights over us than the emigrations of the Danes and Saxons gave to the present authorities of the mother country over England.

Did the Parliament, he asked, have any right to close the Port of Boston? Could it justify, under any written treaty or simply the nature of things, reducing the city from opulence to beggary because of the actions of a few who were already subject to the laws of their own colony? Did it have any right to impose the Stamp Tax or the Townshend duties?

Scarcely have our minds been able to emerge from the astonishments into which one stroke of parliamentary thunder has involved us, before another, more heavy and more alarming is fallen on us. Single acts of tyranny may be ascribed to the accidental opinion of a day, but a series of oppressions, begun at a distinguished period and pursued unalterably through every stage of ministers, too plainly prove a deliberate, systematical plan of reducing us to slavery.

Although he sounded a conciliatory note at the end, it was all but lost under his denunciation of the King:

Can His Majesty thus put down all law under his feet? Can he erect a power superior to that which erected himself? He has done it indeed by force; but let him remember that force cannot give right. Kings are the servants, not the proprietors of the people. Let not the name of George the Third be a blot on the page of history.

Seeing his words in print made him uneasy. What would happen if a copy found its way to England, to the Parliament, to the King himself?

"Sir, I'm nervous about people reading this," he said, turning to Randolph.

"Why?"

"I wrote it in haste. It's full of inaccuracies. I had no one to consult with."

"The force of your ideas will prevail," said Randolph.

Tom looked up and noticed a man's silhouette against the window.

"I just overheard you, Mr. Jefferson," came a voice from in front of the window. "Your modesty becomes a man of your talents."

Tom recognized the voice as Patrick Henry's. Gaunt, lugubrious, and dressed in black homespun, he wasn't inclined to draw attention to himself until he opened his mouth. He had entered the tavern like a ghost, unseen and unheard until he spoke.

"I wish I had more of the virtue myself, but it doesn't come naturally to me," Henry said with a touch of sarcasm.

"Most virtues come naturally," Tom said.

Under his coat Patrick Henry's frame seemed too big for his body, the result, Tom surmised, of his having been underfed as a child. The son of a poor country judge, he had tried his hand at farming and storekeeping and failed at both. For want of a more lucrative livelihood he turned to practicing law. Like the fiddle at which he excelled, he found he could play the law by ear. Tom never forgot when Henry came into his room at the College of William and Mary, announced that he had read the law for six weeks, and was ready to take the bar exam. When he passed, George Wythe, one of the examiners, was so incensed that he refused to sign Henry's license.

Tom shared his mentor's loathing for shortcuts. He himself had spent a four-year apprenticeship in Wythe's Williamsburg law office before he took the exam. A vague feeling of resentment washed over him as he remembered Henry's announcement, but he kept it to himself.

Randolph turned to the burgess from Hanover. "So, Mr. Henry, what did you think of Mr. Jefferson's paper?"

"Not having read it I can't say." He reached over the punch bowl to fill his cup.

"Mr. Jefferson said he sent you a copy."

Henry furrowed his brow in mock concentration. "Hmm, let me think. I'm afraid I mislaid it. For all I know it may be filed away at the Hanover courthouse."

His dismissal was met with silence.

"However," he continued, catching the stone-like expression on Tom's face, "I don't need to remind you that my views with regard to Great Britain coincide with Mr. Jefferson's."

"Including conciliation?" asked Randolph.

Henry's face turned dark. "Well now, that's another matter. In a few days we have to decide whether or not to hold another General Congress. As far as I'm concerned that decision has already been made—not by us but by our tyrants across the sea."

Henry edged around the table and faced Randolph head-on.

"What have all our resolutions, our addresses, our humble appeals gotten for us? Well, I will tell you. Threats of arrest and deportation, that's what. And denunciations by the King. John Adams told me when we left Philadelphia that all of our appeals would be waste paper in England. And we have yet to hear if the King has deigned to look at our last petition. Does His Majesty think by dragging his feet he will drag down our will? Can't you see, gentlemen, that conciliation is a pipe dream, that we have no choice but to take up arms?"

Randolph held up the newspaper in his hand. "Mr. Henry, did you see this? The *Virginia Gazette*--it just came out." Randolph spread the newspaper in front of him and read out loud:

March 18, 1775. London…. The petition from the American Congress to the King has just been presented to His Majesty by Lord Dartmouth, and the same shall be laid before both houses of Parliament at their next meeting.

"Here, see for yourself," Randolph said, handing the newspaper to Henry. "That's not all. I just received a letter from Dr. Franklin, our agent in London, who said the King graciously received our petition. That's the word he used—*graciously.*"

Randolph pushed back from the table and looked up at Henry. "Remember, fools rush in where angels fear to tread."

"Did you make that up?"

"It comes from Pope."

"The Pope?"

"Alexander Pope, the English poet. It might profit you to read him."

To read *anything*, thought Tom.

CHAPTER TWO

Richmond – March 23, 1775

"Resolved, that Thomas Jefferson, Esq., be appointed a Deputy to represent this colony in General Congress."
—Minutes of the Virginia Convention, March 1775

It was Thursday morning, the 23rd of March, a mild, clear day, and a soft breeze was blowing through the courtyard of St. John's Church. Passing through the gate in the brick wall, Tom caught a glimpse of the James River and fall line to the south where the soil-rich Tidewater plantations merged into the crystalline rock formations of the Piedmont. A crowd was forming outside the white clapboard building, some vying for places at the open windows. A British Union Jack hovered over the front door.

Tom entered the church and took a seat by an open window. The pews in the tiny sanctuary barely held the one hundred twenty Virginia farmers, lawyers, shopkeepers, tradesmen and other persons chosen by their home counties to meet in convention. Their object was to weigh London's response to actions the General Congress in Philadelphia had taken the previous fall. Contrasting odors of powder and perfume and sweat filled the room. The bright-colored silks and satins of the wealthy Tidewater planters blazed in relief against the brown and black homespun of the western delegates.

At the center of the platform stood the Reverend Selden's great wooden chair which the Honorable Peyton Randolph was about to occupy as the presiding officer. To the right stood a green baize-covered clerk's table topped by a silver inkwell and quill.

Randolph, pushing his enormous stomach ahead of him, mounted the platform with great effort and heaved himself into the president's chair. His powdered wig was lost in the expanse of his face. He turned to the clerk, a thin-faced little man with a pointed nose, and said, "Mr. Tazewell will read the minutes of yesterday's meeting."

The convention was in its fourth day. Most of the time had been spent plowing through reports from Virginia's delegation to the General Congress. It was enough to make one's head spin. Fifty-six delegates from twelve colonies had met at Carpenter's Hall on September 5, 1774. In a series of declarations they had set forth the colonists' rights, including the right to "life, liberty and property," and cited thirteen acts of Parliament since 1763 as violations of those rights. They had formed a continental association to boycott imports from Great Britain and declared an embargo on all exports to England, Ireland and the West Indies starting September 1, 1775, if the dispute between the colonies and the mother country wasn't resolved by then. A conciliatory address to the King was sent, then an "Address to the People of Great Britain" which, it was rumored, had a profound impact on the British people. Seven weeks later Congress adjourned, agreeing to meet the following May if necessary.

Tom looked around the sanctuary. A vague feeling of guilt came over him when he saw the seven delegates who had gone to Philadelphia, leaving behind their plantations and their families…Peyton Randolph, whose rotund presence in the president's chair exuded dignity and reserve…Benjamin Harrison in the front pew facing him, just as fat and red-faced as Randolph but temperamentally the opposite; his love of food, wine and laughter which he had amply demonstrated in Philadelphia inspired John Adams, a delegate from Massachusetts, to call him "the Falstaff of the Congress"… Edmund Pendleton beside him in the front pew, a thin, pious-looking gentleman from Caroline County; the contrast between them was almost comical—Harrison with his puffy cheeks and perpetual grin waiting for an excuse to break into laughter, Pendleton in his black coat and white wig nestled on his narrow head, looking more like a Quaker preacher than a Tidewater planter...Richard Bland in the second row, adjusting his eye shade to shield out the light; a scholar of constitutional law, he was two months short of his sixty-fifth birthday, the oldest of the Virginians who had gone to Philadelphia. His parchment face looked much like the ancient charters and compacts he studied so much.

Against the wall stood Richard Henry Lee. During the reports he had done most of the talking. His smooth and mellifluous voice, his polished diction and flawless gestures had earned him the title "the Cicero of Virginia." Tom studied him carefully. His profile resembled that of an ancient Roman senator: the high slanted forehead, the Caesarian nose, the narrow aristocratic mouth and chin— the whole contour noble, severe, humorless.

Tom gazed over to the left where Patrick Henry sat, dressed in the same black homespun he'd had on at Mrs. Younghusband's tavern. He remembered what Henry said about the colonies taking up arms, but during the first three days at St. John's Church Henry hadn't spoken a word. Tom could see the boredom on his face.

Across from Henry sat Colonel George Washington of Fairfax County. He too had been silent through the proceedings, but he had such enormous presence that his silence filled the room fuller than most men's speeches. His resolute eyes, his large decisive nose and firm mouth marked him as a natural leader, a man of action if not of words.

The clerk concluded his reading of the minutes:

Resolved unanimously, that the warmest thanks of this convention be presented to the worthy delegates deputed by the former convention to represent this colony in the General Congress, for their cheerful undertaking and faithful discharge of the very important trust reposed in them.

Patrick Henry suppressed a yawn.

Randolph launched into the day's agenda. "I have here," he said, "a petition from the assembly of Jamaica addressed to His Majesty the King, December 28, 1774."

The delegates settled back as Randolph read the petition voicing that British colony's support of American rights. More and more people throughout the empire were beginning to see the justice of the American cause.

Edmund Pendleton of Caroline County rose to acknowledge the petition. "Mr. President, I should like to move that the thanks of this convention be presented to that very respectable assembly, and that it be assured of our most ardent wish to see a speedy return to those halcyon days when we lived a free and happy people."

"Nonsense!" Patrick Henry exploded. There was an audible stir, a craning of necks to see who had violated the assembly's decorum.

Peyton Randolph rapped his gavel. "The delegate from Caroline will continue."

"I move that this resolution be transmitted to the speaker of the Jamaica Assembly," Pendleton said, and he sat down.

The motion was seconded. Randolph recognized the delegate from Hanover County.

"Mr. President," Henry said, drawing in his breath, "I want to propose an amendment to the motion made by my colleague from Caroline." He took a slip of paper from his pocket and read: "Resolved, that this colony immediately be put into a state of defense, and that a committee be appointed to prepare a plan for arming and disciplining such a number of men as may be sufficient for that purpose."

Cries of protest filled the room. Above the voices Tom heard Richard Henry Lee shout a second to the Henry's motion.

Robert Carter Nicholas, a delegate from James City, stood up.

"Mr. President," he said, straining to be heard, "this amendment is not only out-of-place but impious!"

Randolph rapped his gavel again. "Proceed, Mr. Nicholas."

"Is the spirit of these resolutions so lost on Mr. Henry that he responds by calling us to arms?" Nicholas continued.

Benjamin Harrison rose from the front pew, the grin from his face gone. "There is no doubt in my mind of Mr. Henry's purpose," he said. "He would have us believe we are at war with Great Britain, that there is no hope of resolving our grievances peacefully."

Richard Bland tipped his eyeshade, straining to see. "Does he pay no heed to the news from London? Hasn't the King shown his relent by graciously receiving our petition?"

Tom wondered if anyone besides Lee would support Henry's motion.

Edmund Pendleton rose again and faced the delegates. "Gentlemen," he said, "the sympathies of the British people are on our side. The friends of American liberty in Parliament are with us." He turned to look at Henry. "Is this a time to disgust our friends, to extinguish the sympathies that are working in our favor, to turn their friendships into hatred, their pity into revenge? What is there in the situation of the colony to tempt us to do this? Are we a great military people? Are we ready for war? Where are our stores, our arms, our soldiers, our generals, our money? In truth we are poor, we are naked, we are defenseless. And yet we talk of assuming the front of war, and assuming it against a nation—one of the most formidable in the world!"

The speaker turned to Peyton Randolph. "The measure may be brave, Mr. President, but it is the bravery of madmen. There will be time enough to resort to measures of despair, when every well-founded hope has entirely vanished."

Pendleton sat down to a scattering of applause.

"Mr. President!" The room fell silent as Patrick Henry stood up again. "No man thinks more highly than I do of the patriotism and abilities of these very worthy gentlemen. But different men often see the same subject in different lights. I hope, therefore, that it will not be thought disrespectful if I might speak my sentiments freely and without reserve."

Henry placed both bands firmly on the pew in front of him. "The question before this house is one of awful moment to this country. For my own part it is considered nothing less than a question of freedom or slavery. Should I keep back my opinions at such a time through fear of giving offense, I should consider myself guilty of treason."

"So speak your mind!" Randolph was impatient.

"Mr. President," Henry continued, "it is natural for men to indulge in the illusions of hope. We are apt to shut our eyes against a painful truth—and listen to the song of that siren until she transforms us into beasts. Is this the part of wise men, engaged in a great and arduous struggle for liberty?"

Henry left his pew and started to the front. "I have but one lamp by which my feet are guided, and that is the lamp of experience. I know no way of judging the future but by the past. And judging by the past, I wish to know what there has been in the conduct of the British ministry for the last ten years to justify our hopes?"

He turned to Peyton Randolph. "Trust it not, sir; it will prove a snare to your feet. Suffer not yourself to be betrayed with a kiss. Ask yourself how this gracious reception of our petition comports with those warlike preparations which cover our waters and darken our land. Are fleets and armies necessary to a work of conciliation? Have we shown ourselves so unwilling to be reconciled that force must be called in to win back our love? Let us not deceive ourselves. These are the implements of war and subjugation—the last arguments to which kings resort."

Richard Bland removed his eyeshade.

"Our petitions have been slighted," Henry continued, "our supplications have been disregarded, and we have been spurned with contempt from the foot of the throne. In vain, after all these things, may we indulge the fond hope of peace and reconciliation. If we wish to be free we must fight! —I repeat it sir, we must fight! An appeal to arms and to the God of hosts is all that is left us!"

The orator's intensity began to play in the vibrations of his voice.

"They tell us that we are weak—unable to cope with so formidable an adversary. But when shall we be stronger? The battle is not to the strong alone; it is to the vigilant, the active, the brave. There is no retreat but in submission and slavery! Our chains are forged. Their clanking may be heard on the plains of Boston! The war is inevitable. Let it come! I repeat it sir, let it come!"

The veins in Henry's neck stood out like whipcords. The walls of the little church seemed to shake with the vibration of his voice. "Gentlemen may cry peace, peace—but there is no peace. The next gale that sweeps from the north will bring to our ears the clash of resounding arms! Our brethren are already in the field! Why stand we here idle? What is it that we wish? Is life so dear, or peace so sweet, as to be purchased at the price of chains and slavery?"

Henry raised his eyes and hands to the ceiling. "Forbid it, Almighty God!" He paused while the words reverberated between the walls. Then he turned and faced the delegates in the front pew. "I know not what course others may take," he said, his voice barely a whisper, "but as for me, give me liberty—or give me death."

Henry sat down to stunned silence. Through the open window at his side Tom heard the words, "Let me be buried at this spot!" He leaned back in his seat deeply moved, a little exalted, a little sick.

Henry's motion to arm the colony passed by five votes. Robert Carter Nicholas moved to raise an army of ten thousand men. Randolph overruled the motion, but the effect of Henry's speech was clear. The committee to draw up Henry's plan of organization included Nicholas, Harrison and Pendleton. Calling for infantries of sixty-eight and cavalry troops of thirty to be raised by each county, their plan was approved without dissent. Each member was to be equipped with a firelock, bayonet, one pound of gunpowder, four pounds of lead balls, a hunting shirt, and a tomahawk.

Henry's motion forced the convention into a second week. By Monday, the 27th, half the delegates had gone home; the crowds in the courtyard had disappeared. It was decided to convene a second General Congress in Philadelphia on May 10. The same delegates who had gone the first time would be going again with Peyton Randolph to remain at their head. The vote had been unanimous.

A motion to adjourn was on the floor. But Randolph had one more announcement. "In case the Governor convenes the House of Burgesses during the General Congress," he said, "I will have to preside in Williamsburg. A provision should be made to send someone to Philadelphia in my place. I would like to recommend Mr. Jefferson from Albemarle County."

Four days later the next *Gazette* was out. Tom turned to the proceedings from St. John's Church and read near the bottom:

Resolved, that Thomas Jefferson, Esq., be appointed a Deputy to represent this colony in General Congress, in the room of the Hon. Peyton Randolph, Esq., in case of the non-attendance of the said Peyton Randolph, Esquire.

And so it was that Thomas Jefferson, the thirty-one-year-old burgess from Albemarle County, received his summons to history. Half the delegates at the Richmond convention hadn't bothered to stick around. The half that did had no clue about the importance of what they had done. They were ready to go home.

The biggest news from the convention was Patrick Henry's speech; it was the buzz all over Virginia. In Culpeper County, seventy miles to the north, young men scrawled across their hunting shirts the words "Liberty or Death." The orator from Hanover was the hero of the hour while Tom Jefferson, the obscure young delegate from Albemarle County, vanished to his little mountain.

CHAPTER THREE

Monticello – Spring 1775

"All my wishes end where I hope my days will end, at Monticello."
—Thomas Jefferson

Lord Dunmore, the royal governor of Virginia, raced from one blunder to another. On March 28, the day after the convention adjourned in Richmond, he issued a proclamation forbidding the appointment of delegates to the General Congress. On the night of April 20, he ordered an armed company from the *Magdalen*, a British war vessel on the James, to confiscate the colony's gunpowder from the public magazine in Williamsburg. A wave of fury swept through the colony; in Williamsburg people took down their muskets vowing to march on the Governor's Palace.

At Monticello the first blossoms opened on the dogwood trees. A late frost had damaged the grapevines on the back slope, but Tom made sure there was still a good supply of Madeira in the cellar. In the stable under the north terrace Allycrocker was about to foal a colt by Young Fearnought. And "King George," the Monticello blacksmith, was forging nails for the new octagonal wing of the main building.

From the promenade above the north terrace Tom surveyed the scene around him. To the east his eyes gazed over an expanse of forest that rolled into the horizon. In the valley to the north lay the village of Charlottesville, like a cluster of pearls in a sea of emeralds. To the west, over the treetops, the morning sun fell on a mountain wall of lavender and blue.

Was there any other place, Tom asked himself, where nature spread so rich a mantle under the eye? Where else could one look down on the workhouse of nature and see her clouds, her hail, her rain, her thunder all fabricated at one's feet? With what serenity one could rise here above the storms!

A soft, melodic voice broke his contemplation. "The view from here is majestic, isn't it?"

Tom turned around. The eyes that met his were large and luminous, hazel-colored like chestnuts. Her auburn hair, drawn back into curls, revealed a delicate, well-carved face. Tom called her Patty. To the house servants at Monticello, she was Miss Martha, to the outside world Mrs. Jefferson. He drew her to his side and felt her lithe, exquisite form in the embrace of his arm.

"All my wishes end where I hope my days will end," he said, "at Monticello."

"We'll end them here together," she said.

Tom looked toward the house. "Where are my daughters?"

"*Your* daughters?" Patty squeezed his arm. "Don't forget I bore them into the world."

Martha—Patsy they called her—was the older of the two girls, named after her mother. In the two-and-a-half years since her birth, the mother's health had been cause for anxiety. Patsy herself almost didn't make it to her second month, until a breast of milk from Ursula, the wet nurse, revived her. Her baby sister, Jane, had an even more difficult time of it and a year later was still prone to high fever.

"Well, then, where are *our* daughters? I want them to know their father is back."

"Patsy is with her cousin Peter checking on Allycrocker. Ursula is nursing Jane in the girls' bedroom. Did I tell you she'll have to give her up soon? She's in circumstances again."

"So 'King George' is about to expand his dynasty! I must go and congratulate him."

Patty pulled him back.

"Before you do, Tom, please tell me what happened in Richmond."

Tom usually avoided talking politics at home, and he did so with Patty only when she pressed him.

"Did anyone comment on your paper?" she asked.

"What paper?"

"The one you sent Peyton Randolph, your cousin."

"My mother's cousin."

"Well, what did your mother's cousin have to say?"

Tom turned and gazed out from the veranda. "He said tamer sentiments were preferred."

"What about Patrick Henry?"

"He didn't read it."

"But didn't you send him a copy?"

"I did."

"So?"

"He said he mislaid it."

"Mislaid it?"

"I think he was just too lazy to read it."

Patty nodded and compressed her lips. "I remember those books you gave him, when was it, a year ago last fall—"

"—Hume's essays, two volumes. He promised to read them that winter. In the spring he gave them back, said he couldn't get halfway into them."

Patty laughed, two notes high in her throat.

Tom's face turned dark. "Patrick Henry is the laziest man for reading I have ever known. He reads nothing, he writes nothing. He's ignorant—all tongue, no head. Where he gets that torrent of language from is inconceivable."

Patty was silent for a moment. "When are you going to Philadelphia, Tom?"

He met her gaze head on.

"I read the *Gazette* too, you know," she said. "How else am I to keep track of you while you're away?"

"It depends on Governor Dunmore. If he calls the House of Burgesses into session, Cousin Peyton will have to come back and I'll have to replace him—God forbid!"

"I don't understand you, Tom," she said.

"What do you mean?"

"You write the most eloquent protest against the Parliament and King, yet you're content to let others go to Philadelphia."

"Don't you want me to stay home?"

"I'm not answering that. But why are you determined to do one thing and not the other?"

"I don't know, Patty. I can't seem to get my head and heart together. One tells me to go, the other to stay."

He stroked her hair as he did frequently when he was troubled.

"There's nothing I want more than to spend the rest of my days here in peace with you and the children and banish every desire of hearing what goes on in the world. But these are enormous times we're living in. What happens between us and England the next few months will determine how our children live. It's up to us to resolve this conflict. There isn't a person living who is up to it. To tell you the truth, I'm frightened."

Patty broke away and looked at him in mock admonishment. Tom knew that he was being too grave again.

"Well, maybe next time you'll stay home and heed Dr. Gilmer's advice," she said.

"Advice?"

"To guard against passions like fright—and anger. You worked yourself into a white heat when you wrote those resolutions. It's no wonder you didn't make it to Williamsburg."

Tom laughed. "Oh, that life were so simple! Stay home, and the ills of the world will be cured, along with my dysentery. I wish Dr. Gilmer could apply his remedy to the British Parliament!"

The couple's attention was drawn to Ursula, a black woman with a plump round face and generous bosom, as she came out on the terrace holding the baby.

"I heard you mention Dr. Gilmer, ma'am," she said. "Maybe I should send King George to fetch him? Baby Jane has a fever again."

Tom caught an apprehensive glance from his wife, reached out and felt the baby's forehead.

"Yes, please send for him. By the way, Ursula, congratulations! I just heard the good news."

Patty returned with Ursula and Jane back into the house. Tom busied himself on his morning rounds, stopping at the kiln and the nailery where he congratulated King George and calculated how many bricks he needed to complete the house:

NE walls and partitions of parlor 77½ F. in length, to raise the story, 82,000 bricks. SE walls to raise the story, 40,000, whole, to raise the second story, 63,000.

He checked on Allycrocker in her stable where Patsy and Peter were keeping vigil and returned to the house under the north terrace. He stepped into the wine cellar and set aside six dozen bottles of Madeira marked *1767*. He reached for a piece of charcoal and wrote on a slate above the shelf, "FOR DR SMALL."

Eleven years had passed since his old professor and companion from his college days had gone back to England. The last Tom heard from him he was working on a new-fangled steam engine at Matthew Boulton's plant in the English Midlands.

Early that afternoon Dr. George Gilmer came to call, wearing the lieutenant's emblem of the Albemarle militia. Tom knew the instant his friend got off his horse that something was wrong. With barely a greeting the doctor proceeded to examine little Jane. "Keep her on breast milk for two more weeks," he said. "If her fever comes up again, wrap a wet blanket around her."

Tom walked him back to his horse. "Are you sure you can't stay?" he said. "If I can't tempt you with sassafras tea, how about some Antigua rum. My last bottle."

Jokes about the British embargo were making the rounds, but Gilmer was in no mood for humor.

"Tom," he said, "did you see the *Gazette* that came today?"

"No, not yet. Why?"

Gilmer reached into his travel bag. "Read this." He handed him the paper. "There, in the middle column."

Tom read:

Wednesday, April 19 ... To all friends of American liberty, be it known that this morning, before the break of day, a brigade consisting of about 1000 or 1200 men landed at Phipp's farm at Cambridge, Massachusetts, and marched to Lexington where they found a company of our colony militia in arms, upon whom they fired without any provocation and killed six men and wounded four others.

Tom felt the blood drain from his face. He looked up at Gilmer and back at the words, dazed, unbelieving. When he finally spoke, his voice was flat and dry. "So, the sword is drawn."

Gilmer mounted his horse. "We just called up the Albemarle militia. As soon as we get word from Colonel Washington, we're marching to Williamsburg to get our gunpowder back." He looked directly at Tom. "I don't know about you, sir, but I'm ready to put my life on the line." With a salute, Gilmer reined his horse around and galloped down the mountain.

Later that week Tom watched through his telescope while the Albemarle militia, toting flintlocks and bayonets, filed into Charlottesville. Across their green hunting shirts were scrawled the words "Liberty or Death."

He returned to the house through the north passage. When he passed the wine cellar, he remembered the bottles of wine he had set aside for Dr. Small and directed a servant to crate them for shipping.

Back in his library, he reached for a pen.

May 7, 1775 [he wrote]. *To Dr. William Small, Birmingham, England. I send you three dozen bottles of Madeira, being half of a present which I had laid by for you ... Within this week we have received the unhappy news of an action of considerable magnitude between the King's troops and our brethren of Boston … This accident has cut off our last hope of reconciliation … I shall still hope that amidst public dissension private friendship may be preserved inviolate.*

He sealed the letter, not knowing whether he would ever see his friend again.

For the next three weeks the pastoral routine at Monticello continued unabated. Much to her parents' relief, little Jane's fever went down again, but there was still a grayish hue in her skin that warned all was not yet well. Allycrocker had her colt, a thriving future mount for the master of Monticello. His name, Caractacus—after an ancient British king who fought against the invading Romans—sounded just right for the newest son of the first equine family of Albemarle County.

Until the call went out from Lord Dunmore for the House of Burgesses to meet on the first of June, the only news to cause any flurry was that of Patrick Henry's high-handed attempt to recover the stolen gunpowder. Before Colonel Washington had given his order to march, Henry had put himself at the head of the Hanover militia and proceeded to Williamsburg to confront the governor. Before he reached the capital, Carter Braxton, a burgess from King William County, sent 300 pounds by courier to pay for the powder, and bloodshed was averted. But Dunmore, determined to have the last word, issued a proclamation declaring Henry an outlaw. When Henry finally got around to leaving for Philadelphia, a number of his followers accompanied him as an armed guard until he got safely out of Virginia.

The convening of the House of Burgesses meant that Tom would have to take Peyton Randolph's place in the General Congress. While Randolph hurried back to Williamsburg, Tom bade goodbye to Patty and the children.

"I'm going to Williamsburg first," he announced. "I want to see what Dunmore is up to."

"How long will you be in Philadelphia?"

"A fortnight at the most."

"Then promise you'll come home?"

"I promise."

His servant Richard waited outside with his phaeton. Tom kissed his wife and children and waved back at them until they vanished from the crest of the mountain.

Two days later Peyton Randolph met him at the Raleigh Tavern. He looked pale and sounded tired when he spoke. "No sooner do I get to Philadelphia and I have to turn around and come back—for this." He handed Tom a sheet of paper.

"A 'conciliatory proposition' Dunmore calls it, from the Prime Minister. Lord North says any colony that contributes *voluntarily* to defend the empire and support its own government won't have to pay taxes. But there's a hitch: the contributions have to meet Parliament's approval."

Tom was incredulous. "That solves nothing. It only changes the form of the oppression."

"Precisely. That's why I want you to draft the reply. If you don't, I'm afraid Robert Carter Nicholas will. His mind isn't up to the times."

Before Tom's reply could be presented to Lord Dunmore, events in Williamsburg moved at breakneck speed. On the fifth day of the assembly three men sent to investigate the public magazine were wounded by a booby trap put there at Dunmore's order. Once again, the militia prepared to march. Dunmore scooped up his family and personal effects and fled by moonlight to the British man-of-war *Fowey* off Yorktown.

Four days later Archibald Cary, a burgess from Chesterfield County, read Tom's reply to Dunmore's empty chair:

The British Parliament has no right to intermeddle with the support of civil government in the colonies. For us, not for them, has government been instituted here.

The cause of Virginia, he further asserted, was the cause of all of British America:

We consider ourselves as bound in honor, as well as interest, to share one general fate with our sister colonies; and would hold ourselves base deserters of that union to which we have acceded, were we to agree on any measures distinct and apart from them.

Tom climbed back into his phaeton, ready to leave for Philadelphia. Peyton Randolph wanted one more word with him.

"Take your reply to the Congress," he said. "When they see how it harmonizes with their sentiments, they might use it for their own reply."

He added with sly smile: "I also want them to see the latest accomplishment of the author of the *Summary View*."

Casually, Randolph informed Tom as to how his paper had surfaced in Philadelphia in a new printed edition and later found its way to England where it "procured him the honor"—as Randolph put it—of having his name listed in a bill of attainder in the Parliament.

Thomas Jefferson was now an outlaw of the British government.

He turned his phaeton to the north. If there was still a bridge of reconciliation left after his reply to the Prime Minister, he had burned it behind him in Williamsburg. Now he had another, more perilous, rendezvous to keep. There was no turning back.

CHAPTER FOUR

Philadelphia – June 20, 1775

"America is a great, unwieldy body."
—John Adams

Except for the new red brick shops and boarding houses, the scene around him was familiar enough: the cobbled streets, the lanterns, the black-handled water pumps. A few blocks to the right he recognized the white sails of the merchant ships converging and parting over the banks of the Delaware. Even the street names— Pine, Spruce, Locust, Walnut— came back to him as his phaeton rumbled up Fifth Street late in the afternoon of June 20, 1775.

It hardly seemed that nine years had passed since he had last come to Philadelphia as a twenty-three-year-old law student. That time it was to be inoculated against smallpox. This time it was to take his place as Virginia's newest delegate to the General Congress. Each in its own way posed a life risk.

With a population of thirty thousand the city was the largest in the American colonies, but it had the look and feel of an armed camp. He passed an open field where a crowd had gathered to watch a rifle company break rank on command, fire into a dirt mound, and fall back in line in razor precision. In a factory yard the Quaker Blues, with tomahawks under their belts, were practicing their manual of arms. When he reached the yard of the Pennsylvania State House, he spotted the cockaded hats and bucktails of the Philadelphia Associators drilling their battalions behind the brick wall.

Just beyond the yard, on his left, stood the State House, a stately red brick building on Chestnut Street that housed the colony's legislative assembly. Tom caught a glimpse of it before he turned in the opposite direction on

Chestnut. A block-and-a-half ahead, on his left, stood a two-story brick house with a sign over the door that said "Benjamin Randolph, Cabinet-Maker." He sent Richard to quarter his horses at Jacob Hiltzheimer's stable across the street and knocked on the door.

A man with a ruffled shirt and specks of sawdust on his leather apron answered the door. Like Peyton Randolph, he was a distant cousin of Tom's—or thought to be—and had received word that Tom would be replacing Peyton as a house guest.* Randolph showed Tom to his second story room overlooking Chestnut Street. Against the wall stood a luxurious mahogany desk. Tom ran his hand admiringly across the top.

"My latest handiwork," said Tom's landlord.

"A fine piece it is, Mr. Randolph."

Tom looked through the window and caught a glimpse of the State House.

"What do I owe you for a fortnight?"

"Three pounds, sir."

Tom noted the transaction in his account book.

After the seven-day journey it was good to see familiar faces that night. At the elegant new City Tavern on Second Street, he joined his Virginia colleagues for a feast of roast duck, ham and beef, plates of curds and creams and custards, whipped syllabubs, grapes and Madeira wine. Except for Patrick Henry who arrived one week late after the gunpowder episode, all of Tom's fellow delegates had been in town since Congress had reconvened six weeks before.

After dinner, Benjamin Harrison swiped his napkin across his face.

"I don't know if I'll leave this city alive," he said jovially, "but if I die may it be here at the City Tavern."

Richard Henry Lee was in a sullen mood.

"Whether or not we die, Ben, our feasting days

*No evidence has been found that they were related.

are about over. We have enough work to keep us here another month."

The news from Lexington had brought a sense of urgency to the Congress. Within the past week it had taken measures to raise a continental army of twenty thousand, assigning quotas to each of the colonies, and on June 15, after a brief partisan struggle, had elected Colonel George Washington of Virginia as commander-in-chief. Now the most pressing question before the delegates was how to pay for the army.

The only good news to reach Philadelphia in the last month—good for the radicals at least—had been the capture of Fort Ticonderoga by Colonels Ethan Allen of New Hampshire and Benedict Arnold of Connecticut. Now the way was open for a drive into Canada, they said. Allen, so the story went, arrived first, leading his one hundred Green Mountain boys into the fort with sword drawn, demanding the British surrender "in the name of the Great Jehovah and the Continental Congress!" But the conservatives disavowed Allen's action and rammed through a resolution declaring that "this Congress has nothing more in view than the defense of these colonies."

Lee's Roman profile looked more severe than usual against the candlelight. "Here we are, trying to assemble an army," he said. "We've got the British army to rout out of Boston. We've got officers to commission, regulations to write, supplies to collect, money to raise. And we're still wasting time with petitions and resolutions and other puerilities. At this moment John Dickinson is drafting another petition to the King. Apparently, we didn't learn our lesson the last time."

Tom reached into his coat. "Speaking of petitions, I have another one for you—my reply to Lord North on behalf of the House of Burgesses. Peyton Randolph said the Congress might want to make use of it."

Lee took the paper from his colleague across the table. "Wouldn't you know," he grumbled, "I'm on the committee for this one too."

The next morning Tom walked the block-and-half from his lodgings to the Pennsylvania State House. The Pennsylvania Assembly had lent their meeting room at the east end for the second Congress. The building was not only twice as large as Carpenters Hall where the first Congress had met, but it was the official home of a great province and therefore the logical setting for such a body. Tom gazed at the stately red brick building set back from the sidewalk along Chestnut Street. A white square clock tower loomed behind it. On each side a piazza extended out to a smaller wing.

Tom entered the hallway of the main building. Immediately his eye caught the symmetry of the rooms on either side. On his right was the Supreme Court Chamber, on his left the meeting room of the Pennsylvania Assembly. At the rear of the hall a balustrade staircase led to a second-floor room that spanned the width of the building. He looked through the double doors into the grey-paneled assembly room. At the far end were twin fireplaces faced in marble; the president's table, on a low dais, faced the room from the center. Scattered around the floor were thirteen rectangular tables covered with green baize. It wasn't an elegant room, but it had a certain air of nobility, auspiciousness, and at this hour of the morning it was still comparatively cool. Above the din of voices, he could hear the flies from Hiltzheimer's stable banging against the windowpanes.

A few of the delegates were already seated. Others were still coming in or milling about the room. Some Tom had met the night before at the City Tavern. The Rutledge brothers, John and Edward, looked like strutting cavaliers as they made their way to South Carolina's table. At twenty-five Edward was the youngest delegate on the floor. At New York's table sat John Jay, the next youngest delegate at twenty-nine, and short, squint-eyed James Duane trimming the point of his ink-quill. Beside him stood Philip Livingston, a bluff, rotund, irritable-looking gentleman whom Duane seemed deliberately to ignore. Tom couldn't help but notice Caesar Rodney of Delaware; he was by far the oddest-looking man there: tall, thin, pale, with a face not much bigger than a large apple. At Pennsylvania's table sat thin, shadowy John Dickinson, his arms folded resolutely, his face pale as ashes.

Presently Benjamin Franklin entered the room. Tom felt a sense of excitement as the celebrated old man walked slowly to his chair, cane in hand, nodding to his fellow delegates as he passed by. Just returned from England, he was the one man who knew the riddle of the ministry there first hand, who had met Lord North face-to-face, a man wise in the ways of courts and empires. In his brown Quaker suit, his long gray hair trailing over his shoulders, he was the picture of philosophic tranquility.

Tom started toward a table on the right where he spotted Benjamin Harrison and other members of the Virginia delegation. Behind him Richard Henry Lee called his name. At his side was a short man with a round bald head and protruding stomach. His tiny legs and feet seemed to dangle under him.

"Tom, this is John Adams of Massachusetts. He's been asking about you ever since he heard you were coming."

The two men bowed.

In spite of his mismatched physique, the older man's penetrating blue eyes conveyed a keen intelligence. His thin, well-defined mouth suggested a certain clarity, boldness.

"My compliments, Mr. Jefferson, on your paper. What was it called again? *A Summary View of the Rights of British America.* Yes, that's it." There was a touch of envy in his voice. "Perhaps you heard it was published in Philadelphia. It's a masterful work."

Tom felt a flush rise to his cheeks. He hadn't expected anyone in Philadelphia to compliment him on it, much less know that he had written it.

"I'm in total accord with your argument," Adams continued. "The emigration of our ancestors from England gives her no more rights over us than their ancestors had over them when they settled in England. There is no link between us but the King. Any authority that Parliament presumes over us is therefore null and void."

Tom smiled. "That just about sums it up, Mr. Adams. Until now the only one I could get to agree with me was my old law teacher, Mr. Wythe."

John Hancock, who had replaced Tom's cousin Peyton Randolph at the president's table when the latter was summoned back to Williamsburg, rapped his gavel on the president's table and ordered the delegates to their seats. Adams hurried to get one more word in.

"At four o'clock the new commander-in-chief is reviewing his troops in the State House yard. Why don't we go out and have a look after we adjourn?"

Tom agreed, and the two men took their seats. At nine o'clock President Hancock called on Charles Thomson, a thin man with deep set eyes and hair cut short above the ears, to read the credentials of Virginia's newest delegate to the Congress. Hancock asked Tom to stand, and remarked with a strained smile: "We both got to where we are today because of Peyton Randolph."

The son of a Puritan clergyman from Braintree, Massachusetts, Hancock had left home when his father died and become the sole heir to an uncle's vast shipping enterprise in Boston. He was reputed to be the wealthiest man in New England. His face was pale and drawn, but his dark eyes and angular nose and chin suggested that he had once been quite handsome.

Harrison leaned over and whispered to Tom.

"How old do you suppose he is?"

"Fifty?"

"Try again."

"Fifty-five?"

"Thirty-eight."

"Is that what Lexington did to him?"

Tom was half in jest, but there was nothing funny about Hancock's narrow escape on the night of April 18. The Massachusetts delegates were still buzzing about it. Samuel Adams was with him when the British advanced there from Cambridge. Had it not been for a frantic horseback ride by a Boston silversmith named Paul Revere to warn them they were coming the two would surely now be sitting in chains in the Tower of London.

"Actually, it's gout," replied Harrison. "Half the room is afflicted with it. Hancock, Franklin, Phil Livingston, Dickinson, even young Ned Rutledge—they all have it." Harrison leaned closer, affecting a confidential tone. "The real reason we're here is to defend our right to eat and drink and not be taxed for it."

Tom pursed his lips. At least Harrison enjoyed his own humor.

Patrick Henry took the floor and kept it most of the morning. Announcing that General Washington had placed "sundry queries" in his hands, he demanded immediate answers to all of them. "In two days, the General sets out for Boston to take command of the troops. For God's sake, where is his money, his arms, his ammunition? Is he to rely on Divine Providence alone for sustenance?"

Henry pleaded, implored, harangued, inspired. The debate wore into the afternoon. Finally, a committee was appointed to settle the queries, leaving the all-important question of money still unsettled. At four o'clock Hancock adjourned the delegates, and Henry stalked out of the room.

Adams watched him leave as he ambled over to Tom's table. "Every delegate here considers himself an orator, a critic, a statesman, and thinks he has to prove his greatness on every question."

"Mr. Henry is accustomed to getting his way," said Tom, gathering up his notes.

"Well, I know the frustration. The trouble is we are all strangers here. We don't know each other's language, ideas, views, designs. We're jealous of each other, and a little fearful."

"But how can so much debate produce so little?"

"America is a great, unwieldy body, Mr. Jefferson. It's like a large fleet sailing under convoy. The fleetest sailors must wait for the dullest and slowest."

Tom got up from the table. "Can you venture when the dullest and slowest will catch up? I promised my wife that I would leave here in a fortnight."

The conversation halted. Adams's eyes riveted on John Dickinson who was about to pass them in the aisle on his way out. Dickinson caught Adams's glare, stopped as though he were about to say something, flushed, and walked out the door. Adams watched him leave and mumbled: "That's two promises broken, my friend."

CHAPTER FIVE

Philadelphia – June 21-23, 1775

"From this day I date my fall and the ruin of my reputation."
—*General George Washington, June 23, 1775*

I n the State House yard the Philadelphia Fife and Drum Corps burst into a rousing march. Hundreds of spectators scrambled for vantage points along the brick wall. At the south end of the yard, across Walnut Street, prisoners gazed down from their barred windows at the city jail, some holding out wooden poles with sacks at the ends. One by one the Philadelphia Associators, the Quaker Blues, the Silk Stocking Company, the local militia filed through the gate on Walnut Street, past the cannons inside the brick wall, each saluting in succession as they passed before their new commander-in-chief.

Mounted on his white horse, General Washington looked every inch a hero. A long steel sword glistened at his side. His rich gold epaulets shimmered from the shoulders of his blue and buff coat. Behind him the First City Troop of Philadelphia stood motionless, the silver bands on their black hats gleaming in the sunlight. An air of awe and reverence swept through the crowd as the commander-in-chief solemnly returned each salute. Tom watched from the doorway of the State House tower, Adams at his side.

"Such is the pride and pomp of war," observed Adams. There was a curious mixture of envy and cynicism in his voice. He motioned to a brick tower at the east side of the yard. "There's Hancock, over there with Dr. Franklin…wishing, no doubt, that he was the one sitting on that white horse."

"Why is that?" Tom asked.

"Vanity…simple, childlike vanity. It dies hard, Mr. Jefferson. "The good Lord knows I have my share of it.

But Hancock—I've known him since the cradle—he has the most obstinate case I've ever seen."

"Oh?" Tom looked at the older man, waiting for an explanation.

"It was Hancock, you see, not Washington, who wanted to be commander-in-chief. He actually expected it, was quite put out when he didn't get it." A mischievous grin formed on Adams' lips. "You should have seen the mortified look on his face when I nominated Washington. He listened with visible pleasure while I was making my speech, and when I finally came around to describing Washington as my choice"—Adams could not suppress a laugh now—"I never saw a more sudden change of countenance. His jaw dropped a mile."

Tom was perplexed. "Why did you nominate Washington when the British are encamped in Boston? It seems to me that Hancock, who's from Boston—"

"That's just it!" Adams interrupted. "Washington is a Southerner. You see, we Bostonians—all of us from New England in fact—are a highly suspect lot. Dickinson, Duane, John Jay, the others from the middle colonies don't trust us. They think we'd declare ourselves independent tomorrow if we had our way."

"So would you?" Tom asked bluntly.

Adams paused. "I once had hopes of conciliation. But the cancer is too deeply rooted and too far spread to be cured short of cutting it out entirely."

"Yet we're still negotiating."

"I dread it like death, but we can't avoid it. Refusing to go along with Dickinson and his crowd would result in total disunion."

"Even his petition to the King?" Tom pressed.

Adams' face turned red.

"An act of imbecility! It embarrasses every exertion we have made here. Dickinson thinks the Ministry and Parliament will draw back as soon as they hear about the battle at Lexington. But we shall have nothing from them but deceit and hostility and fire and sword!"

Adams pulled a handkerchief from his coat and wiped the sweat from his forehead. "My heart bleeds for the people in Boston, imprisoned in their walls by the British army. God knows what plunders and cruelties they're being exposed to. And mark my word, Mr. Jefferson. The British won't stop there. They intend to make prisoners of all of us, just like those wretched souls across the street begging for coins with bags on their sticks. Prisoners and beggars: that's what we'll become if Dickinson and his deluded followers have their way."

Adams watched General Washington exchange salutes with the Quaker Blues. "We're between hawk and buzzard here, Mr. Jefferson. We're holding the sword in one hand and the olive branch in the other. Yet when all is said and done—" Adams sputtered and shook his head. "Well, you get my drift."

Spurred by the sight of the assembled troops, the committee appointed to consider General Washington's queries met into the night. The next day it proposed a measure on the all-important money question:

Resolved [Secretary Thomson wrote in the minutes], *that a sum not exceeding two millions of Spanish milled dollars be emitted by the Congress in bills of credit, for the defense of America.*

The measure came just in time. The next morning, Friday the 23rd, the commander-in-chief, accompanied by his new aide-de-camp, Major Thomas Mifflin, and his third and fourth in command, Major Generals Charles Lee and Philip Schuyler, set out for the camp near Boston. Tom rose early with the other delegates to accompany them out of the city. In spite of dark clouds that threatened in the north, hundreds of men, women and children lined the dusty road out of the city, waving and cheering as the big Virginian rode majestically by on his white horse. John Hancock and Patrick Henry held stubbornly to their places beside him. Behind them the First City Troop marched in razor-sharp formation. The fifes played, the drums beat, the local militia sang a hastily-composed ballad:

We have a bold commander, who fears not sword nor gun,
The second Alexander——his name is Washington.
His men are all collected, and ready for the fray.
To fight they are directed—for North Americay.

As the procession moved northward, the crowds and cheering diminished, the first crack of thunder rumbled down from the north, and the first block of delegates turned back to the State House. When only a few scattered spectators remained, Hancock dropped out too, complaining of gout.

Tom himself was about to turn back when a ball of dust appeared on the road several hundred yards ahead. Soon he heard the sound of horses' hoofs. Then the rider appeared in full view, his body caked in mud from head to foot. He pulled back on his reins.

General Washington motioned the procession to a halt; Henry, at his side, barked the order to those behind. The rider identified himself as a courier sent down from Connecticut where he had been given a message to relay to General Washington. He handed the General an envelope.

Washington opened it and read the message. His face tightened. He folded the paper, calmly put it back in the envelope, and instructed the courier to carry it to President Hancock.

He turned to Patrick Henry.

"Remember, Mr. Henry, what I now tell you." His voice was barely audible. "From this day I date my fall and the ruin of my reputation."

* * *

Inside the State House, the fever-pitched voices of Richard Henry Lee and John Jay were competing against the storm. Quietly, Tom resumed his seat between Harrison and Lee's empty chair,

Harrison filled him in. "They're arguing over what to call a resolution."

"A resolution?"

"From Dr. Franklin...declaring the causes of our taking up arms. Lee calls it a manifesto, Jay a declaration."

Jay, the more insistent of the two, won out.

Lee sat down, his face beaming.

Tom was puzzled. "You look like you won the argument, Mr. Lee."

"Actually, I prefer 'declaration' myself," Lee replied. "But now Jay thinks he won. It will keep him quiet for a few days."

Tom knew of the hostility between the two men. Lee had spoken of the twenty-nine-year-old Jay as "a young upstart, ambitious above his talents," "intolerably conceited," "equally vociferous on all issues large and small."

Lee's opinion of him had been formed on the first day of the Congress when Jay had opposed a motion to open it with prayer on the grounds that the delegates were so divided in religious sentiments that they could not possibly join in the same act of worship. Tom had heard how Samuel Adams, John's cousin, saved the day when he got up and declared that he was no bigot, that he could hear a prayer from any gentleman of piety and virtue who was at the same time a friend to his country.

Secretary Thomson read back the names of the five delegates appointed to draw up the declaration: John Rutledge of South Carolina, William Livingston of New Jersey, Benjamin Franklin of Pennsylvania, John Jay of New York, and Thomas Johnson of Maryland.

Harrison was pleased. "It was William Livingston, you know, who wrote the *Address to the People of Great Britain* last fall."

"No, I didn't know that," Tom said.

At four o'clock Patrick Henry, the last to return after riding out with General Washington, moved for adjournment.

"Did Hancock get the message the General sent him?" he asked, getting up from the table.

"A courier came in, dripping wet, about two hours ago," Lee replied.

"That's the one."

"Then he got it. Why, do you know what it was?"

"No. But he said something about his reputation being ruined. God only knows what he was talking about."

"Come to think of it," said Harrison, heaving out of his chair, "Hancock has been pretty quiet the last few hours, hasn't looked very good either. Maybe it's his gout." He rubbed his hip. "It acts up every time it rains."

Saturday came and Hancock said nothing about the courier's message. The committee appointed to draw up the *Declaration on Taking Arms* presented its report. John Rutledge, who had been up all night working on it, argued that a copy should be dispatched at once to General Washington. John Dickinson objected; more time was needed, he said, to do justice to such an important document. The debate wore on and Hancock, unable to get a consensus, tabled the matter until Monday.

That night Tom knew that he was going to have to break his promise to Patty. Sitting at his desk at the Randolph's, he thought about what John Adams had said about breaking promises and about the long hot hours in the State House where his colleagues in the Congress endlessly bickered and debated. His first four days in the Congress had seemed like four weeks. He wondered how much longer it would remain in session, how much longer he would have to stay. A month? Six weeks? What should he tell Patty?

He hadn't heard from her since he left home. He wondered how Patsy and cousin Peter were getting along. He worried about little Jane and her fever. And Patty. How he ached to be with her, back on his mountain instead of in a cramped room in Philadelphia where people lived on top of one another, where pigs and chickens wallowed in the gutters, where rancid odors of tar and fish and rotten fruit hung constantly in the air. After dining at the City Tavern, he had hurried back to his room to avoid the deadly miasma the night air sucked out of the stagnant ponds around the city.

When the clock in the State House tower struck eleven, Tom sensed for the first time the stillness of the city. He undressed and went to bed and tried to imagine himself at Monticello, holding Patty in his arms, listening to the crickets on the hillside.

But the stillness here was unnatural, ominous. Tom couldn't put out of his mind the shouting of the company commanders drilling their men, the marching, the firing of the muskets, the playing of the fifes and drums in the State House yard, the cheering of the crowds along the procession route. Then he remembered the courier riding out of the dust and the look on Washington's face when he read the message handed him and his remark to Patrick Henry. A vague, unsettled feeling came over him. He turned over and closed his eyes.

A few minutes later he heard a knock on the door. It was a messenger, sent by President Hancock. "All delegates are summoned to the Massachusetts headquarters," he gasped. "The president says it's urgent."

Without waiting for Tom to reply, the messenger turned on his heels and left.

CHAPTER SIX

Philadelphia – June 24-26, 1775

"The war is now heartily entered into without a prospect of accommodation."
—*Thomas Jefferson to his brother-in-law Francis Eppes*

I t was midnight when Tom arrived. The Massachusetts headquarters, a stately, red-brick mansion on Second Street, stood opposite the City Tavern, where the last revelers were starting for home

John Adams let him in the front door.

"We just got an express from Boston," he said in a hoarse voice. "My worst fears are realized."

He motioned to Hancock halfway up the staircase.

A sheet of paper crackled in Hancock's hand. When he began to speak, he strained to suppress his fury. He told first about the courier coming down from Connecticut "with a rumor of a battle near Boston" on the peninsula of Charlestown, just across the Charles River. There weren't any details, he said. Indeed, he didn't know whether it was a victory or a defeat for the Americans.

But the dispatch that came tonight told the whole story. On the night of June 16, American militia in Boston had sent a detachment of twelve hundred men to seize Bunker Hill. Instead, they built a redoubt on Breed's Hill closer to the city. They worked quietly through the night. At daybreak British warships anchored below discovered them and opened fire. Flaming hotshot flew over the peninsula. Two ground attacks followed with field guns and bayonets. Within a few hours the British had driven out the militia, burned three hundred buildings, and taken the peninsula. The Americans, who had resisted valiantly until they ran out of gunpowder, lost four hundred men. British casualties numbered about a thousand. The next morning, when the first courier left Boston, the Americans were priming for another attack.

When Hancock finished, Tom still wasn't certain who had won. True, the British had borne the brunt of the casualties. But the Americans had not only failed to rout them out of Boston; Charlestown, too, was in British hands, reduced to a pile of ashes. Of one thing he was certain: the Ministry and Parliament meant to drive the colonists into submission by force, whatever the cost. To reason with them was hopeless. All those humble petitions and appeals sent overseas might as well have been waste paper, just as John Adams said. Even the battle at Lexington hadn't changed their minds.

Hancock folded the paper, trying to think of something to say to break the stunned silence.

Adams swiped his handkerchief across his mouth and blurted: "Apparently there are some people in New York and Philadelphia to whom a ship is dearer than a city, and a few barrels of flour dearer than a thousand lives."

Gradually the shock turned to anger. Vows of revenge ricocheted across the room. Samuel Adams edged over to his cousin John and declared, "Governor Gage will have to answer to the fatal consequences of this attack."

Hancock raised his hands to quiet the delegates, but it wasn't any use. When it was quiet enough to be heard Samuel Adams spoke up again, his voice curiously calm but firm. "Whatever our recourse, we can't jeopardize our brothers and sisters in Boston. Retaliation in itself will defeat our purpose. It must serve the public good."

Hancock couldn't contain himself any longer. "Burn Boston," he cried, "and make John Hancock a beggar if the public good requires it!"

John Adams seized his cousin by the arm. "We've got work to do, Sam'l—Hancock too when he cools down. We've got to collect all the powder and saltpeter we can and send it to Boston—tonight."

Tom started back to his lodgings. All that he had read about the rise and fall of empires came back to him with shattering force. When men failed by other means to free themselves from the grip of tyrants, had they any choice but to draw the sword and sever the hand? Wasn't that the one great lesson of history so often repeated? His whole body felt clammy and chilled. Back at his desk above the cabinet maker's shop, he reached for his quill. To George Gilmer, his friend and lieutenant of the Albemarle militia, he wrote: "As our enemies have found we can reason like men, so let us show them we can fight like men!"

* * *

Monday, June 26. A shaft of morning sunlight poured into the Assembly Room, splashing an eerie bluish hue on the gray-paneled wall at the rear of the room. Against the glare John Dickinson looked more than ever like a ghost. On the near side of the room, John Jay, James Duane and the other New York delegates sat rigid and silent, carefully avoiding the eyes that were fixed on them.

President Hancock finished rereading the express. He passed it to the clerk and heaved a sigh of fatigue: "After we received the news, three of the Massachusetts delegates—the two Adamses and myself—went out to beg gunpowder from the Committee of Safety of this city. That was at one o'clock. By three o'clock we had rounded up ninety quarter casks. At sunrise they were en route to Boston."

But it wasn't enough, John Adams insisted. More gunpowder and saltpeter had to be manufactured and shipped to Boston, a committee appointed, directions published.

The discussion droned into the morning. A few of the delegates started writing letters. Doctor Franklin, his chair pulled into the aisle, was panning a reading glass over the *Pennsylvania Gazette*. Tom reached for a sheet of paper to write his brother-in-law:

To Francis Eppes, Esquire, Monday, June 26. Dear Sir: You will before this have heard that the war is now heartily entered into without a prospect of accommodation. Washington set out here on Friday last as Generalissimo of all the Provincial troops. We are extremely anxious till we hear of his arrival at Boston.

The debate resumed on the *Declaration on Taking Arms*. Tom looked at Doctor Franklin again, sitting contemplatively in his chair, the *Pennsylvania Gazette* folded across his lap. Until a few nights ago the two had exchanged but one or two pleasantries on the assembly room floor. But thanks to a dinner for the combined delegates at the City Tavern (a Saturday night tradition, Tom found out, that had started during the first Congress) the two had finally been able to talk one-on-one.

"I read your instructions for the Virginia delegates," Franklin said that night. "What was the title again? Yes, a *Summary View of the Rights of British America*. John Adams gave me a copy, told me of your reputation for literature and talent for composition. After reading your booklet I concur with his judgment."

Franklin's manner was grave and subdued. When he removed his bifocals, Tom saw for the first time the hollowness in his eyes. When the conversation turned to his illegitimate son, William, Tom felt as though he was looking all the way into them.

"Ninety-seven pages I wrote him," Franklin said. "It occupied most of my voyage back from London." He sat hunched over, his hands cocked over his cane. His eyes fastened on the bifocals dangling from his fingers. "I told him everything, how I tried to get Parliament to repeal the Tea Act, even offering to pay from my own pocket for the tea that was thrown into Boston Harbor, how all my overtures for reconciliation failed, why I thought he should resign his appointment from the King. Then as soon as I got off the ship, I heard the news from Lexington."

It pained Tom to see the old philosopher-statesman, the colonies' most revered citizen, reduced to a broken old man. Franklin loved William as much as any father could love his son. As a boy, in 1752, William had stood beside his father when the latter raised his kite into the thunderclouds to prove that lightning was electricity. Franklin dreaded the ridicule that so often attended his scientific experiments. But his son couldn't have been prouder than he was that day. Eleven years later, in 1763, the father was equally proud when his son was appointed by King George III to be the royal governor of New Jersey. William had held the post ever since.

Franklin's letter had been to no avail. William, determined to remain loyal to the crown, was already packing up to sail in reverse the course his father had sailed from England.

Tom placed his hand on the old man's arm.

"For whatever it's worth, Dr. Franklin, the defection in your family isn't unique. I have a relative too, although not so close as a son, but close as a friend. His name is John Randolph, a cousin on my mother's side and the younger brother of the speaker of our House of Burgesses. He's 'going home' too, as he puts it.

"John and I grew up together," Tom continued. "We shared an interest in a great many things—books, gardening, music. When the late Francis Fauquier was our governor, we played the violin together at his palace. He played with such grace and dexterity. His violin was the finest I had ever seen—a Cremona, 1660."

How vividly Tom remembered those days as he stared out the window into the State House yard and the agreement they had made—when was it? four years ago—in the hope that he would one day inherit his cousin's violin. The agreement decreed that if Tom died first, John would inherit 100 sterling worth of Tom's books. If his cousin died first, Tom would inherit his violin. It was all very official, signed and sealed in the General Court at

Williamsburg. George Wythe and Patrick Henry had been the witnesses. Tom wondered what would come of his bargain with John. If he went back to England would his violin go too? To lose a friend was bad enough. But a 1660 Cremona!

Tom felt a nudge. "I don't mean to interrupt your reverie," said Benjamin Harrison seated next to him, "but congratulations."

"Congratulations? For what?"

"Your first appointment."

"First appointment...to what?"

"The committee to rewrite John Rutledge's declaration on arming."

"Oh." All Tom could think about was going home.

"It was Dr. Franklin's doing. But no matter. You'll soon wish you were back in Virginia."

"No more than I do now. Why?"

"Mr. Dickinson was appointed too, at his own request."

CHAPTER SEVEN

Philadelphia – Late June, 1775

"To oppose (the King's) arms we also have taken up arms."
—Thomas Jefferson's draft of the Declaration of the Causes of
Taking up Arms, *June 1775*

After Congress adjourned for the day, Tom waited in the corridor to find out where the committee charged with rewriting Rutledge's declaration would be meeting. William Livingston of New Jersey tapped him on the shoulder. "I just spoke with Mr. Dickinson," he said. "He's invited us to his home tonight."

Tom looked at the tall, plain man dressed in black. The two had been introduced only briefly the week before. There was nothing elegant or genteel about him, but Tom remembered what Benjamin Harrison said about him afterwards: "It was William Livingston, you know, who wrote the *Address to the People of Great Britain.*"

One might wonder what thought crossed Tom's mind at that moment. Would Livingston be willing to rewrite Rutledge's draft? But what if Dr. Franklin had other plans? What if he wanted Tom to do it? How could he turn him down? But to accept would all but guarantee he would break his promise to Patty.

Tom addressed the older delegate cautiously. "Sir, I hope you don't think it presumptuous of me, but I wonder if you would consider rewriting Mr. Rutledge's declaration."

"We are but new acquaintances. Why are you asking *me?*"

"Because one of my Virginia colleagues told me you drew up the *Address to the People of Great Britain.*"

Livingston gave him a bewildered look. "Oh no, sir, I'm afraid you're mistaken. It was Mr. Jay, not I, who drew up that document."

Tom mumbled an apology while Livingston politely excused himself.

That evening, on Monday the 26th, the committee met at Dickinson's home. Just as Tom had feared, Dr. Franklin persuaded the committee to assign him the task of rewriting Rutledge's declaration. Their consent was unanimous; neither Dickinson nor Jay nor Rutledge himself objected.

Back at his lodgings, Tom wondered if anyone on the committee apart from Dr. Franklin had read his *Summary View of the Rights of British America*. Otherwise, how would they have assented to quickly to his suggestion? Had they known of his opposition to Parliament's authority over the colonies, wouldn't they have picked someone else to argue the grounds for armed resistance? Or was Franklin's reputation such that no one questioned his choice? Five days after his arrival in Congress, Tom felt honored at being handed this assignment, but he couldn't help but feel the irony of it too.

The next morning dawned wet and cold. Tom hurried across Chestnut Street to the State House. Entering the building, he stamped the water off his shoes and heard two angry voices in the corridor outside the assembly room. He looked up and saw John Jay jam his finger into Richard Henry Lee's chest. At that moment Jay's eyes met Tom's; he seized the button of Lee's coat and led the older man over to him.

"I understand, sir," Jay said, "that this gentleman informed you that William Livingston drew up the *Address to the People of Great Britain*.

"Oh no, sir. That information didn't come from Mr. Lee. It came from another Virginian."

Jay turned back to Lee who rolled his eyes. It appeared Jay was about to apologize when he said, "Never mind," and disappeared into the assembly room.

Lee turned to Tom and asked, "So who was the other Virginian?"

"Mr. Harrison."

"It figures. What a buffoon, getting things fouled up as usual. You know what John Adams calls him, don't you? 'Sir John Falstaff,' of no use in Congress or committee but a great embarrassment to both."

Tom ignored the slight of his colleague. "I wonder how he got the idea that Livingston wrote that address?"

"I was on the committee with Livingston and Jay. They wanted me to write it which I did. Neither one liked it so Jay took it and rewrote it himself. It was horrendous. The language was infantile, the whole case for our grievances pusillanimous and disgusting. Livingston, who was the chairman, had the dubious honor of presenting it on the floor."

"So that's what led Harrison into the error."

That night Tom went to work on the new declaration. Staring out his window he wondered how to assimilate everything that had been said during the debate on Rutledge's draft, how to sift the grain from the chaff, how to find common ground in the quagmire of conflicting views and vested interests and transform it into a forceful, cohesive statement. The committee had told him to take his time, not rush through the job as Rutledge had done. When he finished the first draft, he started on the second, carefully interlining, deleting, writing in alternate words and phrases and crossing out those he didn't like. Three nights later he was finished. He turned back to the front page and read his charges against the Ministry and Parliament:

They have undertaken to give and grant our money without our consent...They have cut off the commercial intercourse of whole colonies with foreign countries...They have extended the jurisdiction of courts of admiralty beyond their ancient limits...By one act they have suspended the powers of one American legislature, and by another have declared they may legislate for us themselves in all cases whatsoever ...

Toward these deadly injuries from the tender plant of liberty…we have pursued every temperate, every respectful measure. We have supplicated our king at various times, in terms almost disgraceful to freedom.

Even Congress's boycott of British imports had failed. Certainly, the British government knew how much the colonies were suffering because of it. But didn't the ashes at Charlestown make it clear how the king's army was going to respond?

To oppose his arms we also have taken up arms.

Tom knew this was nothing less than a declaration of war. Two months ago, he never dreamed that such a document would have to be written, let alone that he would be the one to write it. Yet here it was in its terrible reality, declaring the one alternative the colonies had left.

He laid the paper down. He was angry, but this time he felt nothing of the illness which had come over him after he poured out his rage in the *Summary View*. Writing this paper had cleared his brain. He felt confident, exhilarated. There wasn't any question now about what the colonies had to do. And he had spelled out the reasons as forcefully and convincingly as he could. Although he admitted it to no one, he was pleased with the job he had done.

The next afternoon the committee reassembled to hear what he had written. Tom nervously followed the others up the balustrade staircase in the tower room to the committee chamber on the second floor. Three paned windows admitted a glare of sunlight into the walnut-paneled room. He sat down and laid his paper on the table.

A few minutes later his nervousness vanished. Benjamin Franklin, his bifocals off and his hand resting over his eyes, nodded in rhythm while Tom repeated his charges against King George III and Parliament. Rutledge smiled too broadly to show that he had buried his resentment. John Jay sat with a fixed gaze, his expression revealing nothing. Livingston shook his head. Dickinson's face grew tight, his body rigid as though he were about to rise from his chair.

But it was Livingston who spoke first. "It's no better than Rutledge's!" he blurted, his tone one of surprise more than disgust.

"Pray tell, what's wrong with it?" asked Dr. Franklin.

"Too much fault-finding and declamation. Our Southern gentlemen seem to think a reiteration of tyranny and despotism is all that is needed to unite us at home and convince the bribed voters of Lord North of the justice of our cause."

Tom felt hammer-struck. A volley of insults flew across the table between Livingston and Rutledge, and Rutledge strutted out of the room. An awkward silence followed.

It was Dickinson's turn to speak. Gravely he rose from his chair, looked at Rutledge disappear through the door, and turned to Tom. "Your paper, Mr. Jefferson, displays some fine qualities and confirms the many compliments I have heard about your pen." His voice was soft, constrained. "However, our colleague from New Jersey is quite right. The charges are severe and offensive. They are dressed in the language of revenge, not conciliation. Do we wish to shut out forever the amicable agreement with Great Britain that we desperately seek?"

A reddish glow wiped the ashenness from Dickinson's face. His thin, cadaverous body seemed to take on a youthful vigor as he warmed to his argument. "For what reason are we taking up arms? Is it for glory or conquest? Is it to carry out a grand design of separation from Great Britain? God forbid! We must assure our brethren across the sea that our only object in this struggle is to recover our rights as free Englishmen. I ask you, where is that assurance?"

Dickinson's eyes panned around the table. "As propaganda at home, gentlemen, this manifesto may unite us, but abroad it will surely destroy us. I therefore cannot accept it, and I shall oppose it with every fiber of my body as I opposed Mr. Rutledge's."

Dickinson sat down. Tom leaned forward, dazed, dumfounded, his eyes fixed downward. What was there to say? Franklin merely raised his eyebrows at the futility of continuing the debate. The Pennsylvania Farmer wielded more influence than anyone else in the State House, and without his approval the declaration would never get out of committee.

There was but one alternative: let Dickinson himself write it. Let him take the document and put it into a form he could approve.

The suggestion was made.

Triumphantly, Dickinson agreed.

"But your petition to the King," Dr. Franklin interjected. "Is it finished?"

"Give me another day or two. Then I will draw up the declaration. I'll have it ready in a week."

The committee adjourned. Tom remained in his chair, staring at the blurred words on his paper. What went wrong? Had he forgotten what John Adams said? Surely there was some misunderstanding. Seven years ago, in his *Letters from a Farmer in Pennsylvania*, Dickinson had done more than anyone to wake up the colonies to the evils of British policy. Yet here he was begging, bargaining, petitioning, delaying—like a child clinging to his mother at the prospect of separation. Why was he holding back? Why did he still desire conciliation when it was obvious the British had no intention of meeting them half way? Why? Was it love? Loyalty? Guilt?

Fear?

When the others left, Dr. Franklin edged around the table with his cane and put his hand on Tom's shoulder. "I think I know how you feel ... angry perhaps ... frustrated ... hurt."

Tom nodded. "And bewildered."

"Aye, by Mr. Dickinson you mean. Why is he not with us? Well, let me tell you something. You have your cousin John Randolph to contend with. I have my son, William. Mr. Dickinson has his mother plus the whole Quaker establishment here in Philadelphia. Just yesterday he told me how they were intimidating his mother and his wife who in turn have been begging him to hold back. His mother said to him, 'Johnny, you will be hanged, your estate will be confiscated, and you will leave your excellent wife a widow and your charming children orphans and beggars.' Indeed, I pity him. From my soul I pity him."

"But sir, you are risking as much as he."

'No…no…I'm in my seventieth year now. For me this dispute will be over soon." He paused, drew in his breath. "Besides, my wife is dead and my son is sailing for London tomorrow. I have only myself to account for."

Tom looked up and saw a tear on the old man's cheek. "One day we'll have to account for each other, sir."

Franklin nodded grimly. "On that you're quite right, my son."

Thomas Jefferson in 1791. *Painted from life by Charles Willson Peale. Independence National Historical Park.*

Peyton Randolph, Thomas Jefferson's distant cousin, was the first president of the Continental Congress. He had a great stomach and a massive red face that seldom smiled or frowned. When he spoke, he sounded like an expiring balloon. *Portrait by John Wollaston. Virginia Historical Society.*

A
SUMMARY VIEW
OF THE
R I G H T S
OF
BRITISH AMERICA.
SET FORTH IN SOME
R E S O L U T I O N S
INTENDED FOR THE
I N S P E C T I O N
OF THE PRESENT
D E L E G A T E S
OF THE
PEOPLE OF VIRGINIA.
NOW IN
C O N V E N T I O N.

By a NATIVE, and MEMBER of the
HOUSE of BURGESSES.
by Thomas Jefferson

WILLIAMSBURG:
Printed by CLEMENTINA RIND.

Thomas Jefferson's proposed resolutions for Virginia's delegates to the First Continental Congress were published—unbeknownst to him—in this 1774 pamphlet, *A Summary View of the Rights of British America*. The consequences would be enormous. *By Thomas Jefferson. Colonial Williamsburg Foundation.*

When George III ascended to the throne in 1760, things were going pretty well for the colonists. Not so by 1774. Wrote Jefferson in his Summary View, "Kings are the servants, not the proprietors of the people." The king didn't like that very much. *Workshop of Allan Ramsey (anonymous). National Portrait Gallery, London.*

Thomas Jefferson barely concealed his resentment of Patrick Henry, who passed his bar exam after six weeks. Jefferson called him "the laziest man for reading I have ever known." *By George Bagby Matthews after Thomas Sully. Colonial Williamsburg Foundation.*

Banished from the capitol in Williamsburg by the royal governor, Virginia's burgesses met in convention—make that undercover—at St. John's Church in Richmond to decide on their next move. *Ticknor Brothers Collection. Boston Public Library.*

Monticello—the home Jefferson built on his little mountain. With what serenity one could rise here above the storms! *By Betty Gordon (1975). Marilee and Milton Nieuwsma Collection.*

Richard Henry Lee, the "Cicero of Virginia," had a gift of gab surpassed only by Patrick Henry's. His profile resembled that of an ancient Roman senator: the high, slanted forehead, the Caesarian nose, the narrow mouth and chin. *By Charles Willson Peale. Smithsonian Institution.*

Colonel George Washington of Fairfax County had such enormous presence that his silence filled the room fuller than most men's speeches. His resolute eyes, large, decisive nose, and firm mouth marked him as a natural leader. *By James Peale after Charles Willson Peale. Independence National Historical Park.*

"Give me liberty, or give me death," proclaimed Patrick Henry at St. John's Church. "Let me be buried at this spot!" responded an eavesdropper outside an open window. *By J.L.G. Ferris. Smithsonian Institution.*

THE

PROCEEDINGS

OF THE

VIRGINIA

CONVENTION

IN THE TOWN OF

RICHMOND

ON THE 23RD OF MARCH

1775

HELD AT SAINT JOHN'S CHURCH

ORIGINAL PUBLICATION COPYRIGHTED IN 1927 BY
ROBERT LECKY, J^R RICHMOND, VIRGINIA
MCMXXXVIII

The Proceedings of the Virginia Convention where Patrick Henry gave his famous speech, overshadowing Thomas Jefferson's summons to history: his appointment as a "deputy" to the Continental Congress. *William & Mary Law School.*

Virginia's royal governor, Lord Dunmore, was prone to blunders. After dissolving the House of Burgesses, he forbade sending delegates to Congress and then seized the colony's gunpowder. Things might have turned out better if Dunmore had done less. *By Sir Joshua Reynolds (1765). Scottish National Gallery.*

An artist's conception of Martha (Patty) Jefferson based on contemporary descriptions. Her eyes were large and luminous, hazel-colored like chestnuts. Her auburn hair, drawn back into curls, revealed a delicate, well-carved face. *By George Geygan (1965). National First Ladies' Library.*

The Colonial Capitol at Williamsburg—home of Virginia's House of Burgesses until Lord Dunmore, the colony's royal governor, unceremoniously dissolved them. *Colonial Williamsburg Foundation.*

Raleigh Tavern in Williamsburg, where the bolder burgesses— Jefferson, Washington, Patrick Henry, and others—reconvened after Dunmore shooed them out of the capitol. *Tichnor Brothers Collection. Boston Public Library.*

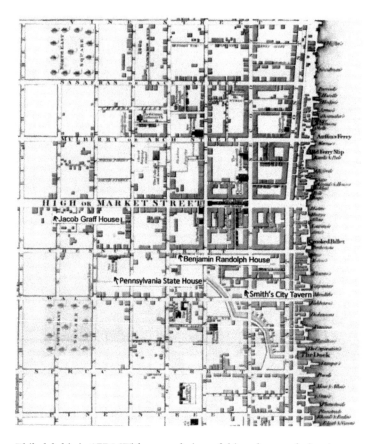

Philadelphia in 1776. With a population of thirty thousand, the city was the largest in the American colonies. Key sites that figure in Jefferson's story are identified. *Detail of map by Benjamin Easburn. Library of Congress.*

The Pennsylvania State House on Chestnut Street, home of the colony's legislative assembly, was the setting for the Second Continental Congress. It's now called Independence Hall. *By Nathaniel Currier and James Merritt Ives. Yale University Art Gallery.*

Daniel Smith's City Tavern on Second Street was a favorite watering hole of delegates to the Continental Congress. *Artist unknown. Historical Society of Pennsylvania.*

The Assembly Room of the Pennsylvania State House. *Independence National Historical Park.*

Benjamin Franklin, the oldest delegate to Congress, had just returned from England. He was the one man who knew the riddle of the ministry there firsthand, who had met Lord North face-to-face, a man wise in the ways of courts and empires. *By Joseph Duplessis (1778). Smithsonian Institution.*

Thomas Jefferson first met John Adams in the Continental Congress in June 1775. The older man's penetrating blue eyes conveyed a keen intelligence. His thin, well-defined mouth suggested a certain clarity, boldness. *By John Trumbull (1793). Smithsonian Institution.*

The son of a Puritan clergyman, John Hancock left home when his father died and inherited an uncle's vast shipping enterprise in Boston. When he took over as president of the Second Continental Congress, he was reputed to be the wealthiest man in New England. *By John Singleton Copley. Massachusetts Historical Society.*

Mounted on his white horse, General Washington looked every inch a hero. His rich gold epaulets shimmered from the shoulders of his blue and buff coat. *By John Faed (1899). Westervelt Warner Museum of American Art.*

Jefferson had just taken his seat in the Continental Congress when he learned of the battle of Bunker Hill. Among the casualties was a physician-turned-general, Dr. Joseph Warren of Boston, a close friend of John Adams. *By John Trumbull. Boston Museum of Fine Arts.*

It was in this cottage, part of Jefferson's half-built mountaintop mansion, that he and his wife Patty spent the first night of their honeymoon on New Year's night, January 1, 1772. *Photograph by David Broad (2013). Thomas Jefferson Foundation.*

As a boy, William Franklin stood beside his father when the latter raised his kite into the thunderclouds to prove that lightning was electricity. Later, as royal governor of New Jersey, he remained a devout loyalist, much to his father's dismay. *Detail from Currier and Ives (1876). Benjamin Franklin Historical Society.*

Launched in 1733, *Poor Richard's Almanack* circulated throughout the colonies, making its creator, Benjamin Franklin, a rich man. *Published by Benjamin Franklin. Library of Congress.*

Greorge Wythe, Jefferson's law mentor, was the most respected lawyer in Virginia. A formidable presence in the courtroom, his gentle manner outside the courtroom could get the surliest dog "to unbend and wag its tail." *By David Silvette (1979). William & Mary Law School.*

 Milton J. Nieuwsma

On May 23, 1776, Jefferson moved into a new apartment building owned by a Philadelphia bricklayer named Jacob Graff. It was in this room that he wrote the Declaration of Independence. His writing box, an eighteenth century version of a laptop computer, is displayed on the table. (See below.) *Top: 1975 reconstruction, National Park Service. Bottom: Smithsonian Institution.*

81

Drafting the Declaration of Independence, Benjamin Franklin and John Adams go over the text with Thomas Jefferson. *Painting by J.L.G. Ferris. Smithsonian Institution.*

Jefferson's first draft of the Declaration of Independence shows minor changes suggested by John Adams and Benjamin Franklin. These included replacing "sacred and undeniable" with "self-evident" in the second paragraph. *Reproduction. Milton and Marilee Nieuwsma Collection.*

John Dickinson stayed loyal to the Mother Country to the bitter end, refusing to vote for independence. He left his place at Pennsylvania's table before President Hancock called for the vote. *Portrait by Charles Willson Peale (1780). Independence National Historical Park.*

On August 2, 1776, an engrossed copy of the Declaration of Independence was laid out for the delegates to sign. Fifty delegates signed that day. Six more signed later, making a total of fifty-six. *National Archives.*

President Hancock ordered a public reading of the Declaration of Independence on July 8. Hundreds of townspeople embraced and cheered in the State House yard while Jefferson's words were read from an observatory tower. *North Wind Picture Archives.*

Milton J. Nieuwsma

Bells throughout the city, including this one in the State House tower, pealed throughout the night. Of all the patriots celebrating independence, Jefferson was probably the least able to enjoy it. He just wanted to go home. *Independence National Historical Park.*

87

CHAPTER EIGHT

Philadelphia – July 1775

"In defense of the freedom that is our birthright, we have taken up arms."
—*Final draft of the* Declaration of the Causes of Taking up Arms, *adopted by Congress, July 6, 1775*

Tom Jefferson wasn't yet born when Benjamin Franklin began publishing *Poor Richard's Almanack*. A potpourri of poems, proverbs, puzzles, weather forecasts and witticisms, the little magazine circulated throughout the colonies and made Poor Richard's creator a rich man. A quarter century later, Franklin quit the magazine to spend more time on his myriad inventions like the lightning rod, bifocals, swim fins, the Franklin stove and a urinary catheter. Believing the general public should freely benefit from these things, he never took out a patent. But he didn't need the money either.

Tom was only fifteen—still an adolescent—when Franklin put Poor Richard to bed for good.* Meanwhile, his sayings had become as familiar in colonial households as lines from *Hamlet* and *As You Like It*. Besides being America's most revered scientist, statesman and inventor, Franklin was America's Shakespeare.

So when he showed up at Smith's City Tavern on Saturday night in early July, an air of celebration filled the room. Tom helped the aging, gout-afflicted doctor to his table and sat down beside him. A dozen or so fellow delegates had already arrived. Others were drifting in.

Benjamin Harrison rose to propose a toast. "If I may quote Poor Richard," he said, raising his glass, "In beer there is proof that God loves us and wants us to be happy."

*Launched in 1733, *Poor Richard's Almanack* ceased publication in 1758.

"I'm flattered you remember his advice," said Franklin, "but don't forget what else he said: 'In beer there is freedom, in wine there is wisdom, in water there is bacteria.'"

When the laughter subsided, John Adams stood up and proposed another toast from Poor Richard: "Search others for their virtues, thyself for thy vices."

"Well said, my friend," rejoined Franklin, "but well done is better than well said."

And so the bantering continued as the delegates, in rare good humor, tried to outdo each other quoting Poor Richard, trying at the same time to impress the author. As Tom listened, he detected a hint of cynicism:

"Three may keep a secret if two of them are dead."

"Love your enemies, for they tell you your faults."

"He that falls in love with himself shall have no rivals."

"Democracy is two wolves and a lamb voting on what they shall have for lunch."

When the bantering ended, Franklin tugged at Tom's sleeve and said, "I have one just for you: 'When the Lord closes a door, he opens a window.'"

"I didn't know you were a man of faith, Dr. Franklin."

"Not many do," Franklin said, adding with a twinkle: "I can't wait to surprise them at heaven's gate."

"So what do you mean, 'When the Lord closes a door?'"

"Yesterday, when the committee rejected your declaration, I knew how hurt you were. But I think it happened for a reason."

"What reason can that be?"

"Your reply to Lord North's so-called conciliatory proposition, the one you wrote for Virginia, remember?"

"Yes, I gave it to Richard Henry Lee. He said he was on the committee to draft the reply for Congress."

"You know what the Prime Minister is trying to do, don't you? By going to each colony separately and not to Congress, he's trying to divide us."

"Did you tell Mr. Lee that?" Tom asked.

"Yes, Mr. Adams too. We're on the same committee. We read your reply for Virginia and want you to reply for Congress. Don't you see? There's your window."

Tom thought about his promise to Patty.

"Look, we need you to write this." Franklin said. "Mr. Dickinson is already working on the new arms declaration, plus he's writing another peace petition to the King. You're the only other member of Congress who can do this justice."

"Why can't *you* write it?" Tom asked boldly.

"I have made it a rule, whenever in my power, to avoid becoming the draftsman of papers to be reviewed by a public body."

"Well, after yesterday I can see why."

Benjamin Harrison, who overheard the exchange, interjected: "Dr. Franklin, if you write the reply, have Poor Richard say something clever."

"That's another reason," Franklin said. "People would be disappointed if he didn't. And they wouldn't take the reply seriously if he did, including the Prime Minister."

Tom sighed. "All right, then. I'll do it."

The following week, as promised, John Dickinson finished his rewrite of the *Declaration on Taking Arms*. After rejecting the two earlier versions by Rutledge and Jefferson, the committee listened wearily as Dickinson read from his draft:

Our forefathers [he began], *inhabitants of the island of Great Britain, left their native land to seek on these shores a residence for civil and religious freedom.*

Two minutes into the reading, Franklin dozed off. He had heard it all before. Some of the words were Tom's, which Dickinson repeated. But one paragraph that stood out was Dickinson's own:

Our cause is just. Our union is perfect. We fight not for glory or for conquest. In our own native land, in defense of the freedom that is our birthright, we have taken up arms.

The committee gave its assent. When Secretary Thomson read the committee's declaration to Congress the next day, July 6, the vote was unanimous. Tom consoled himself that at least some of his ideas had made it into the final draft. In spite of his disdain for Dickinson—or perhaps not realizing that it was Dickinson's version he had just voted on—John Adams called it a "spirited manifesto."

Two days later, on Saturday, July 8, came the moment Adams had been dreading: the final reading of Dickinson's peace petition to the King. "An act of imbecility," he had called it. Tom remembered his pronouncement when they were watching General Washington review his troops in the State House yard. Secretary Thomson began reading Dickinson's words:

Most gracious sovereign: We, your majesty's faithful subjects…entreat your majesty's gracious attention to this our humble petition.

Agitated, Adams got up and headed for the door, brushing past Tom. "I need some air," he mumbled, vanishing out of the room into the yard.

Dickinson immediately followed him out. Tom watched through the open window as Dickinson, the door slamming behind him, called Adams' name. "Give me the reason," he shouted, "why you New Englanders oppose our every measure on reconciliation!"

Tom strained to hear him against the competing voice of Secretary Thomson:

We assure your majesty [the secretary continued] *that notwithstanding the suffering of your loyal colonists, our breasts retain too tender a regard for the kingdom from which we derive our origin….*

"Look ye, Adams! If you don't fall in with our plans, I and my friends will break off from New England."

Your majesty will find your faithful subjects on this continent ready and willing at all times to assent and maintain the rights and interests of your majesty, and of our mother country....

"You're wasting your time, Mr. Dickinson. I am not to be threatened. Let the Congress judge between us."

...That your descendants may govern your dominions with honor to themselves and the happiness of their subjects is our sincere and fervent prayer.

The reading concluded, the delegates gathered at the president's table to sign the document. Whether they agreed with it or not, unity was a must. After Adams signed, he threw down his pen. "Are we for war or for peace?" he snapped. "Dickinson wants it both ways."

Tom intercepted him as he turned away from the table. "Sir, it's been a long week," he said. "Are you joining us at the City Tavern?"

"Not tonight. Lost my appetite. Besides, I owe my wife Abigail a letter, and James Warren, the new president of our Provincial Congress in Massachusetts. I must tell him of our latest folly."

Tom wasn't sure about the wisdom of doing that. With so many British agents lurking around, one could never be certain that a letter from a delegate to Congress wouldn't be opened and inspected, let alone reach its intended recipient.

But he let the moment pass. Besides, he had his own correspondence to catch up on. The Virginia Convention, his colony's counterpart to the Massachusetts Provincial Congress, was about to meet again in Richmond. Back at his apartment, Tom took out his pen and wrote Peyton Randolph on behalf of his fellow Virginians:

Philadelphia, July 11, 1775. Sir: The continued sitting of Congress prevents us from attending our colony convention. The present crisis is so full of danger and uncertainty that a fall Congress will be indispensable.

Meanwhile, the *Declaration on Taking Arms* and Dickinson's Olive Branch Petition—as it came to be called—went off to England on the same ship. *"Ordered,"* Secretary Thomson wrote in the minutes, *"that the above be sent undercover to the king."*

That business done, Tom turned to the task Dr. Franklin had asked him to take on: drafting Congress's reply to Lord North's conciliatory proposition. Staring out the window from his desk, he pondered how to begin and wondered how Franklin had ever talked him into it. His mind drifted to another conversation he'd had with him that week, one that revealed the elder statesman's gift of persuasion, that skillful playing of innocence and intrigue that could get people to act against their will. Franklin described how, before leaving London, he had befriended an unemployed corset maker and freelance journalist who was down on his luck. His name was Thomas Paine. Sensing a reservoir of talent and fire in the young man, Franklin talked him into leaving home and seeking his fortune in Philadelphia. The kindly Franklin even wrote a letter introducing him to his friend Dr. Benjamin Rush. An "ingenious, worthy young man," he called him. It was just the break Paine needed, for he had just been named editor of the *Philadelphia Gazette.*

Once again, Tom read Lord North's proposition, the same one he had replied to for Virginia. But now his task was to reply for *all* the colonies, not just one—and try to outsmart the Prime Minister at his game of divide and conquer. *"Resolved,"* the document from London began, declaring in legalese that any colony contributing to the common defense and the government's administration of justice—read into that *for any rebellion against the Crown—* would be relieved of taxes and duties except those necessary for regulating commerce.

Tom began his response:

Resolved, That the colonies of America are entitled to the sole and exclusive privilege of giving and granting their own money…That they are entitled at all times to enquire into their application….

Even as he wrote, he wondered if the Prime Minister would deign to read his reply after Congress's last two manifestos, whose messages were mixed to say the least, or if he did would he take it seriously, even without Poor Richard to lighten the tone. When he finished, he showed his draft to Dr. Franklin, who scribbled something on a piece of paper. "Here, add this," he said.

Tom took the piece of paper, half expecting it to be a line from Poor Richard but instead found these words:

We are of the opinion that the proposition is altogether unsatisfactory, because it imports only a suggestion of the mode, not a renunciation of the pretended right to tax us.

"The Prime Minister must know we mean business," Franklin said.

***

Monday, July 31, 1775. *"Motion made, and question proposed,"* Secretary Thomson wrote in the minutes. Tom's carefully composed reply and Franklin's scribbled out amendment lay side-by-side on the president's table as Congress debated their fate—"*by paragraphs"* recorded the secretary.

John Adams had had enough. "Juvenilities and puerilities become not a great assembly like this," he said in disgust.

But the motion passed. Unanimously. Once again, unity was a must. Tom's reply to the Prime Minister was now Congress's reply; it answered for all the colonies, not just his.

Maybe Franklin was right. Maybe some things happen for a reason, like the committee rejecting his *Declaration on Taking Arms,* then the Lord opening a window, just like he said. Having been given a second chance, Tom felt relieved, vindicated.

After the vote was taken, he looked over to Franklin. The wise old doctor, his hands folded over his cane, caught his glance. Raising a thumb, he nodded and smiled back.

CHAPTER NINE

Richmond – August 1775

"I hope the returning wisdom of Great Britain will, ere long, put an end to this unnatural contest."
—*Thomas Jefferson to his cousin John Randolph*

Newspapers wasted no time printing Congress's *Declaration on Taking Arms*. From Boston in the north to Savannah in the south, it was read to thundering cheers in the marketplace and recited in fervent prayers from pulpits. General Washington proclaimed it to his applauding troops outside Boston. Yet even now, with Dickinson's Olive Branch Petition on its way to London, Congress was still holding the door open to reconciliation.

The delegates in Congress were exhausted. In the six weeks since receiving the news from Bunker Hill, they had adopted articles of war for the army and established a military hospital with whatever doctors they could recruit. They scoured the country for saltpeter, niter and sulfur for making gunpowder and any muskets that would shoot. They set up a system for military communications, secured loans for army supplies, and printed and put into circulation two millions of paper dollars. A Department of Indian Affairs was organized, an appeal made to the powerful Six Nations to remain neutral in the war: "Brothers, Sachems. Warriors! Open a kind ear! King George, persuaded by wicked counselors, has broken the covenant chair with his children in America."

The debates had dragged on through the scorching heat and pestering flies from Jacob Hiltzheimer's stable. Tempers had flared, nerves worn thin. It had been a slow, frustrating business. Complained Benjamin Harrison, Tom's colleague from Virginia: "It's high time there was an end to it. We have been too long together."

Finally, on Tuesday, August 1, 1775. Secretary Thomson wrote in the minutes: *"Adjourned, to Tuesday the fifth of September next."* Not only had Congress been in session too long, but Tom's fear of having to come back to Philadelphia for another session was going to be realized.

Checking out of his apartment at the Randolph's, he gathered up his horses and phaeton at Hiltzheimer's stable and met Harrison in front of the State House. Accompanied by his servant Richard, they would be making the journey back to Virginia together. But before going home they had business to attend to in Richmond: the third Virginia Convention at St. John's Church, the same place where Patrick Henry had given his "liberty-or-death" speech five months before.

Harrison heaved himself into the carriage and pulled a newspaper from his vest. "Here, read this, Tom," he said. "It's a letter from John Adams to James Warren in Massachusetts. Right there at the top."

Tom took the newspaper from Harrison and read:

In confidence, I am determined to write freely to you at this time. A certain great fortune and piddling genius whose fame has been trumpeted so loudly has given a silly cast to our whole doings.

"Who is he talking about?" Tom asked.

"Who do you think? John Dickinson," Harrison said.

"How did this get into the paper?"

"Read on."

The paper described how the letter's bearer, one Benjamin Hichborn of Massachusetts, had been captured on a ferry between Newport and Providence en route to Boston. An officer from the *Swan*, a British gunboat, seized the letter and gave it to his commander. Next thing it hit the *Massachusetts Gazette* and other Tory newspapers around the colonies. Copies were hawked in the streets of occupied Boston, sung around the British campfires on Bunker Hill. Loyalists and patriots alike read them and laughed or swore according to their allegiances. The letter crossed the ocean, reaching London about the same time as Dickinson's humble petition. Even worse, it lifted the cloak of personal animus that hovered over the Congress. Now the world knew that America wasn't so united after all.

The trip to Richmond would take six days. Most of the road followed Indian trails with wagon ruts on either side. There were rivers to ferriage—six in Pennsylvania alone—and money to exchange as each colony had its own currency. Roadside inns were hot and crowded, often with three people to a bed. Even so, a road-weary traveler was lucky to get a room.

Tom welcomed having Ben Harrison along for the arduous trip home. John Adams could call him what he wanted—profane, obscene, the Falstaff of the Congress, whatever—but Tom found him to be as amiable a traveling companion as one could be. Harrison traced his Virginia roots back to the 1630s when his great-great grandfather started a plantation in Charles County. The first Benjamin served as a clerk for the Royal Governor's Council. The next four Benjamins including the current one served in the House of Burgesses.*

Beneath Ben's jovial veneer Tom detected a residue of sadness. He didn't know why until Ben told him how he had lost his father and baby sister to lightning while closing a bedroom window, leaving Ben at nineteen and the oldest of ten children as the head of the family. "Our friend Dr. Franklin just hadn't invented the lighting rod yet," he said, seeming to shrug off the ancient family tragedy. But Tom could tell it didn't go away.

By and by the conversation turned to their time together in Congress. Top on the list was Dickinson's Olive Branch Petition.

*The Harrison family's public service tradition would extend to two future U.S. presidents, Benjamin's son William Henry and great grandson Benjamin.

"Tom," Harrison said, "did you know we had two debates on his petition?"

"Two debates?"

"Yes, before you came Dickinson had written an earlier version that was even worse than the one we signed. He argued how we needed to offer the Ministry and Parliament the *opportunity*—that's how he put it—to stop the effusion of British blood—*British* blood, mind you—and that the humbler our petition, the more it would help our cause if they rejected it."

"Hmm. Makes sense to me," Tom said.

"But then he objected to the word *Congress.*"

"But he wrote it. How could be object—"

"That's what *doesn't* make sense. He turned to Hancock and said, 'There is but one word in the paper, Mr. President, of which I disapprove, and that is the word *Congress.*' Then I got up and said, 'There is but one word in the paper, Mr. President, of which I *approve*, and that is the word *Congress.*' It didn't bring the house down, but it got a chuckle—even from Mr. Adams."

It was late Sunday afternoon, August 6, when Tom and his traveling companion finally arrived in Richmond. The Virginia Convention was already in session at St. John's Church. The events since March had instilled a sense of urgency among the delegates. Not only were Lexington and Bunker Hill fresh on their minds, but they worried about what mischief Lord Dunmore, the royal governor, would be up to next. From his remote command post on the *Fowey*, he had already tried to confiscate the colony's gunpowder. Now he threatened to burn Williamsburg and free any slaves who fought with the British.

Before Tom arrived, the Convention—with Peyton Randolph back in the president's chair—had established a Committee of Safety to provide a military regiment for each county. Patrick Henry had gotten himself appointed commander of the combined Virginia regiments, which not only freed him from the tedium of Congress but moved him a step closer—at least as Tom saw it—to his fantasy of military glory.

Among the delegates was George Wythe, Tom's old law mentor, representing the City of Williamsburg. At forty-eight, he was the most respected lawyer in Virginia, a formidable presence in the courtroom but whose gentle manner outside the courtroom, it was said, could get the surliest dog to "unbend and wag his tail." Sometimes this approach worked inside the courtroom as well, and he proceeded to teach this by example to his law students.

Tom's mentor approached him in front of the church, a violin case in hand. "Remember, Tom, the bargain you struck with John Randolph? If you died first, he would get 100 sterling worth of your books. If he died first, you would get his violin."

"Yes, of course. You witnessed the agreement. So did Patrick Henry."

"Well, here's his violin. He stopped over to say good bye and asked me to give it to you."

"Good bye?"

"He's leaving for England on the next ship out. He wants to dissolve the agreement. Please don't let Peyton see it. I can't imagine how upset he is about his brother going to England."

Tom caught a glimpse of the speaker entering the church, looking ten years older than he did in the spring. The younger Randolph, with whom he played the violin at the Governor's Palace in their college days, had also been a protégé of Wythe's, but after rising to the post of royal attorney general for the colony of Virginia had chosen to stay loyal to the crown.

"Tom, I have some other bad news," Wythe said. "William and Mary College got word the other day that William Small died."

Tom stared at him in disbelief.

"Putrid fever, or it could have been malaria. They're not sure."

"When?"

"Back in February. In Birmingham, England. You know he went back to work on that newfangled steam engine—"

"—with Matthew Boulton, I know."

Wythe shook his head. "Forty years old. Weren't you his star student?"

"I wouldn't say that. But yes, we did get along well," Tom said. "And he taught me a lot."

Indeed, it was Dr. Small, Tom's classics professor at the College of William and Mary, who had introduced him to the great Enlightenment thinkers like Newton and Bacon and Locke, and instilled in him an appreciation of science and mathematics and natural philosophy. It was also Dr. Small who had introduced him to his friend George Wythe when Tom, then a seventeen-year-old college student, told him he wanted to study law.

Tom remembered the case of Madeira he had set aside for him in his wine cellar and the letter he sent after hearing the news from Lexington. Then it struck him: if Small died in February and the first shot was fired April 19—who could forget the date?—Small would have been dead two months before that happened. At least his friend was spared the knowledge that their two countries were at war.

But now he had another letter to write, this one to John Randolph who was preparing to leave for England himself—not as a native-born Englishman like Small, but as an American-born loyalist, the brother of Peyton Randolph no less, head of the Virginia Convention which was preparing at that moment to arm the colony against the British:

I hope the returning wisdom of Great Britain will, ere long, put an end to this unnatural contest...To me it is of all states but one, the most horrid. My first wish is a restoration of our rights; my second, a return to the happy period when, consistent with duty, I may totally withdraw from the public stage and pass the rest of my days in domestic ease and tranquility, banishing every desire of ever hearing what passes in the world.

It was the 26th of August. The convention had one more piece of unfinished business: electing delegates to the September session of Congress. John Tazewell, the clerk, announced the results:

Peyton Randolph 89
Richard Henry Lee 88
Thomas Jefferson 85
Benjamin Harrison 83
Thomas Nelson, Jr. 66
Richard Bland 61
George Wythe 58

So it was that Tom Jefferson, until now Peyton Randolph's stand-in at the Second Continental Congress, was elected a delegate in his own right. Not only that, his third-place finish—ahead even of Ben Harrison and George Wythe, his old law professor—signaled a rising star on Virginia's political stage.

Still, Tom wished nothing more than to return to Monticello and pass the rest of his days in domestic tranquility, just as he confessed to John Randolph. As he started down Richmond Hill and pointed his phaeton westward, he couldn't imagine the heartbreak that awaited him at home.

CHAPTER TEN

Monticello – September 1775

"We both seem to be steering opposite courses; the success of either lies in the womb of time."
—John Randolph to Thomas Jefferson

Big families were the rule of the day on eighteenth century Virginia plantations, just as they would be on Midwest prairie farms a century later. Peter Jefferson's family was no exception. Tom's father, one of Albemarle County's most prosperous tobacco farmers, had sired ten children with his wife, the former Jane Randolph. She herself had come from one of Virginia's most prominent and prolific families which included her cousin Peyton Randolph, the speaker of Virginia's House of Burgesses, and Peyton's younger brother John, the colony's attorney general. Tom was the third of the ten Jefferson children.

Tom's sister Martha, three years his junior, had married his best friend Dabney Carr, who died of unknown causes—commonly called bilious fever—leaving a widow and six children in Tom's care. Tom carved out a clearing on Monticello's wooded slope to receive his friend's body. The clearing surrounded a great oak tree and became the Jefferson family graveyard.

Some years earlier, in 1765, Tom had lost an older sister, Jane. Unmarried at twenty-five, she too died of bilious fever. But as common as such deaths were in those days—people knew so little about germs, much less how they did their deadly work—her death hit him especially hard. More than siblings, they were soulmates and shared a passion for music.

When Tom and Patty Jefferson's second daughter, Jane, was born in April 1774, they named her after her Randolph grandmother and late aunt Jane. When Tom returned to Monticello after his first stint in the Congress, little Jane was wasting away from another one of those mysterious illnesses. Her symptoms had started in the spring, but neither Ursula's breastmilk nor Dr. Gilmer's ministrations had been of any use. Tom hadn't been home a week when little Jane, at seventeen months of age, died in her weeping mother's arms. It was like she had been waiting for her daddy to come home.

To assuage his grief, not to mention his anxiety over the events unfolding in Boston and London, Tom plunged back into his little world of building and farming. His mountaintop mansion, which began with the building of a one-room cottage at the end of a pavilion, was only half finished. It was in that cottage that the newlywed couple had spent the first night of their honeymoon on New Year's night, January 1, 1772.

Three-and-a-half years later, they were still talking about it. After their wedding at The Forest, Patty's childhood home near Richmond, they set out for Monticello in the soft, romantic snow, comfortably ensconced in their phaeton. By nightfall the snow had turned into a blinding, bone-chilling blizzard. Rising snowdrifts blocked the way. Forced to abandon the carriage, they finished the journey on horseback. It was midnight when they arrived.

While Patty shivered in her cloak, the bridegroom kindled a fire and retrieved a half bottle of wine from behind a stack of books. Soon a roaring blaze lit up the room. The lovers collapsed in front of the fireplace and warmed themselves in each other's arms.

Thus they began married life.

By now the main structure had been built, the red bricks fired by slaves on Monticello's grounds. A large octagonal parlor looked out over the grounds flanked by two unfinished L-shaped pavilions—one leading to the honeymoon cottage, the other to an identical structure on the right. On the east side of the building, a handsome white pillared portico welcomed visitors, while the west entrance facing the grounds—the one the family used—was still a work in progress.

Tom had designed his home in the style of the 16th century Italian architect Andrea Palladio. With fall approaching, his immediate needs were for skilled stonemasons and brickmakers to finish the pavilions. While the house itself was built of brick, most of the stone used for the mantles and columns was imported, because there was no suitable stone to be quarried in Virginia. Tom did manage to find enough stone and a mason named William Rice, an indentured servant, to make eight Doric columns for the west portico. It may well have been the same Mr. Rice who carved the gravestone for little Jane, the first Jefferson to be laid to rest in the family graveyard.

Every night, at sunset, the three remaining family members—Tom and Patty and their three-year-old daughter Patsy—would gather in the parlor and watch the autumn sky turn a radiant red over Monticello's western slope. While Tom and Patty made music—Tom on the violin and Patty on the pianoforte—little Patsy would play on the floor beside them, too young to understand why her little sister wasn't playing there with her.

Tom's new Cremona violin—new at least for him—was the finest of its kind, made by Nicola Amati in 1660. The body bore the Amati trademark of brilliant amber. The finger and tailpiece were ebony, the string pegs, ivory. As for Patty's pianoforte, it had been her engagement present from Tom, the finest money could buy, and the result of a last-minute change-of-mind by her husband-to-be who had first chosen a clavichord. "I have since seen a pianoforte and am charmed by it," Tom had written his agent in London. "Send me this instrument then, instead of the clavichord; let the case be of fine mahogany, solid not veneered, the compass from Double G to F in alt, and plenty of spare strings; and the workmanship of the whole very handsome and worthy of the acceptance of a lady for whom I intend it."

Together they played and sang while Patsy entertained herself on the floor. Among their favorites were Corelli and Haydn and Handel and Vivaldi. Before long an American composer joined their repertoire— Francis Hopkinson, whose popular song "My Days Have Been So Wonderous Free" was making the rounds in colonial parlors:*

My days have been so wonderous free,
the little birds that fly
with careless ease from tree
to tree were but as blest as I.

Ask gliding waters if a tear
of mine increased their stream.
And ask the breathing gales if e'er
I lent a sign to them.

On one such playing, Patty stopped in the middle and began to weep. Patsy looked up from the floor and said, "Why Mommy cry?" Tom put down his violin and laid a comforting hand on her shoulder.

Tom dreaded the day he would have to leave Monticello and go back to Philadelphia. Meanwhile, he received another letter from John Randolph, the former owner of his violin, that reminded him of the importance of family in times of conflict:

Though we may politically differ in sentiments, yet I see no reason why privately we may not cherish the same esteem for each other which formerly subsisted between us. Should any coolness happen between us, I'll take care not to be the first mover of it. We both seem to be steering opposite courses; the success of either lies in the womb of time.

*Coincidentally, Francis Hopkinson would later become a signer of the Declaration of Independence as a delegate from New Jersey.

Congress was getting ready to reconvene. What was Tom to do? Go to Philadelphia by himself? Or take Patty and Patsy with him? He knew Patty was in no condition to make the three-hundred-mile trip over the dirt roads and bridgeless rivers, but he pressed the question anyway.

"Cousin Peyton is taking his wife," he said.

"Let him," she said. "If something happens to me, let it be here in Virginia, not in Philadelphia where I don't know a soul."

"But I can't leave you and Patsy here alone."

"Then we'll stay at The Forest with my sister."

One week passed, and then another. Patty's sister and her husband—Elizabeth and Francis Eppes—arrived at Monticello in a fancy four-wheeled phaeton. Elizabeth helped her pack. A few days later, Tom's wife and daughter, in the back of the Eppes' family carriage, bid him a tearful goodbye and set out down the mountain.

It was high time for Tom to leave. Congress had already been in session for three weeks. Mounting his phaeton, his servant Jupiter in the jump seat behind him, he snapped the horses' reins to begin the journey. When the carriage started moving, he took out his account book and wrote, "*September 25 - Set out from Monticello for Philadelphia.*" One can only imagine what emotions lay beneath the spare inscription. Anxiety over the war? Grief over little Jane's death? Guilt over leaving Patty and Patsy behind?

Turning north at the foot of Monticello, Tom stayed within sight of his beloved Blue Ridge Mountains until they faded into the horizon. Summer rains made the roads more gouged and treacherous than usual. The horses slipped and strained through the mud. As darkness descended, a flash of lightning appeared ahead, followed by the rumble of an approaching thunderstorm.

CHAPTER ELEVEN

Philadelphia – October 1775

"The suspense under which I am is too terrible to be endured."
—Thomas Jefferson to Francis Eppes

It was war all right. The night Tom arrived back in Philadelphia, he learned that John Adams and John Dickinson—that *certain great fortune and piddling genius*—weren't speaking to each other. Over dinner at the City Tavern, Adams described how he had encountered Dickinson on Chestnut Street and how the latter cut him dead. Dickinson's Quaker friends were doing the same while Tory sympathizers rejoiced in the shadows.

Adams took the rejection in stride, even viewing it with pugnacious pride. At last he had said what was in his heart. If the whole world knew, so be it.

"Think of it as a happy accident," Ben Harrison said, raising his glass.

"Think of what?" Tom asked, fatigued after his long trip.

"The capture of Mr. Adams' letter. Don't you see, it's written in the stars."

"What is?"

"Independence. The word is finally out there. Maybe now people will see it in black and white, give them time to grow used to the idea."

Philadelphia wasn't the only battlefront in the war of words. In London—although Congress didn't know it yet—George III's answer to Dickinson's Olive Branch Petition was to declare the American colonies in rebellion. The King hadn't even bothered to read it. Tom's reply to Lord North's so-called conciliatory proposition was likewise ignored. Just as Adams predicted, Congress's appeals would amount to waste paper in England. (The

Olive Branch Petition did make its way to Parliament, which voted it down, 83-33.)

To make matters worse, the British had just launched an assault on Falmouth, just up the coast from Boston. A warship called the *Canceaux* shelled the town from the sea, burning one hundred and fifty buildings to the ground. At the same time, dysentery was sweeping through Washington's troops in Cambridge. Ten thousand men moaned in whatever spaces they could find—stables, barns, sheds, under bushes and fences. A few even deserted. The General's pleadings for clothing, shoes and medicines went unheeded by Congress, which seemed more intent on arguing than acting.

The attack on Falmouth from the sea posed a whole new problem for Congress. How could the Americans defend themselves against the greatest navy in the world?

That wasn't all. "Don't forget we have a constitution to form," Adams reminded his colleagues as they got up to leave the City Tavern. "We have fifteen hundred miles of coastline to fortify, millions to arm and train, a naval power to begin, commerce to regulate, Indian tribes to negotiate with, a standing army of twenty-seven thousand to raise…."

By the time Adams finished his litany, most of his colleagues had left. Exasperated, John plopped a few coins on the table turned to Tom. "Well, I have one piece of good news anyway. Montgomery and Arnold captured Montreal. You know what that means—"

"That Canada will join the union."

"Precisely. If nothing else gives me hope, that does."

Back at his Chestnut Street lodgings, Tom was joined by Peyton Randolph and his wife Elizabeth and another delegate from Virginia, Thomas Nelson, and his wife Lucy. The wives' presence made him miss Patty more than ever, but he knew she was in good hands with her sister and husband at The Forest.

The three-hundred-mile trip from Williamsburg had taken a toll on the Speaker who, Tom remembered, looked like he had aged ten years when he last saw him in Richmond. Now he had aged even more. It was a blessing John Hancock had replaced him as President of Congress; the stress would have been too much. Now he was just another delegate.

Tom was honored to be included with the Randolphs in a Sunday dinner invitation to the home of a Philadelphia wine merchant named Richard Hill. The home stood on a plantation several miles out in the country. The dinner was an elegant affair, filled with lively conversation. After his plate was removed, Peyton Randolph gasped and began to choke. He collapsed onto the floor. Rushing to his aid, Tom and the others watched in helpless panic as his body shook and went limp and shook again. The intervals between each gasp of air grew agonizingly longer until the gasping finally ceased. A doctor who had been summoned declared him dead.

Tom accompanied Randolph's remains, together with Randolph's distraught widow, back to their lodgings on Chestnut Street, and from there to nearby Christ Church where preparations began for his funeral. When Tom returned to his room late that night, he wrote in his account book:

"October 22 — This evening the amiable Peyton Randolph esq. our Speaker died about 9. o'clock of an apoplexy at the house of Mr. Richard Hill."

Two days later, Congress took the day off for the Speaker's funeral. The Reverend Jacob Duché, the Christ Church rector, presided over the service. Every delegate attended, not only to pay respects to the first President of the Continental Congress, but also to be seen at the most prestigious gathering in town. Every delegate wore black crepe around his arm.

***

Back at his lodgings, Tom had set aside one day a week to write home. A month of wearisome debates and committee work had crept by and not one of his letters had been answered. His worries about Patty started up again. On October 31, he dashed off a letter to his friend John Page:

I have set apart nearly one day in every week since I came here to write letters. Notwithstanding this I have never received the scrip of a pen from any mortal breathing.

On November 7, he repeated his complaint to his brother-in-law, Francis Eppes, in a tone no less frantic:

I have never received a scrip of a pen from any mortal in Virginia since I left it, nor been able by any inquiries I could make to hear of my family…The suspense under which I am is too terrible to be endured. If anything has happened, for God's sake let me know it.

Meanwhile, the British were pressing their assault from the sea. In Philadelphia came word that British warships were advancing on Norfolk, threatening to repeat the destruction they had done to Falmouth. Tom feared the ships would turn inland on the James River to Richmond. He urged Patty to remove to a place of refuge until the danger passed, but that plea went unanswered as well.

On Thursday, November 9, Congress finally received George III's answer to the Olive Branch Petition. President Hancock called on Charles Thomson, the secretary, to read the document:

"A proclamation by the King," he started.

The secretary cleared his throat and continued:

Whereas many of our subjects in diverse parts of our colonies and plantations in North America, misled by dangerous and ill-designing men, and forgetting the allegiance which they owe to the power that has protected and supported them, have at length proceeded to open and avowed rebellion…All our officers, civil and military, are obliged to exert their utmost endeavors to suppress such rebellion and to bring the traitors to justice. [signed] *King George III, August 23, 1775.*

Stunned silence fell across the room. The only sounds Tom heard were pigs on Chestnut Street squealing in protest on their way to market. He looked around the room. There was no mistaking John Adams' I-told-you-so expression. Ben Franklin's raised eyebrows signified the futility of dealing with the King. At Pennsylvania's table John Dickinson sat frozen, his eyes fixed on the floor.

To most in Congress, it was no surprise that Parliament rejected Dickinson's Olive Branch Petition. It was the King's refusal to read it that stung, and his proclamation was the last straw.

Back at his lodgings, Tom wrote John Randolph, now back in England, to report on the death of his brother Peyton:

Dear Sir [he began], *I am to give you the melancholy intelligence of the death of our most worthy speaker....*

That wasn't the only reason Tom wrote him. Maybe his cousin's loyalist sympathies would change if he knew the latest development in the north:

Montreal acceded to us on the 13th...In a short time we have reason to hope the delegates of Canada will join us in Congress and complete the American union.

But the main reason he wrote was to vent his feelings about the King:

It is an immense misfortune to the whole empire to have a king of such a disposition at such a time. We are told, and everything proves it true, that he is the bitterest enemy we have....

Believe me, dear sir [he concluded], *there is not in the British empire a man who more cordially loves a union with Great Britain than I do. But by the God that made me, I will cease to exist before I yield to a connection on such terms as the British Parliament proposes, and in this I think I speak the sentiments of America.*

Three days later came devastating news that Ethan Allen, the hero of Ticonderoga, had been taken prisoner in

Montreal. Any illusion the Americans had about Canada joining their cause vanished in that instant. While Congress prepared a public protest, Allen sat in chains on a British vessel on the St. Lawrence River.

Tortured more than ever over his worries about Patty's health—he still hadn't heard a word from her— Tom drafted an appeal for Allen's release. Christmas came and went and Congress failed to act.

No longer could Tom bear the silence, let alone his frustration with Congress. Quietly he bid goodbye to his landlord and retrieved his horses and phaeton from Hiltzheimer's stable. Crossing the river at the edge of town, he noted in his account book, *"Dec. 28 – Pd. ferriage over Schuylkill ¼,"* and set out for home.

CHAPTER TWELVE

Monticello – January 1776

"The blood of the slain, the weeping voice of nature, cries, 'TIS TIME TO PART'."
—*Thomas Paine*, Common Sense

On January 1, 1776, the war came to Virginia. Making good on the British threat to attack Norfolk, Lord Dunmore sent a landing party ashore to torch the wharves and warehouses in the city's port. To make things worse for the revolutionaries, he promised freedom to any slaves who joined the British side. His emancipation proclamation, not destined to rank with Lincoln's, only got the Virginians' dander up more. When George Washington got wind of Dunmore's mischief, he called it "a flaming argument" for separation.

Tom didn't learn of the attack until he arrived at The Forest, the Eppes plantation near Richmond where he had gone to retrieve his wife and daughter. The disturbing news from Norfolk was more than offset by Tom's relief to find Patty alive if not in the best of health. The Eppes family had indeed taken good care of her. But to this day Patty's silence during her husband's three-month sojourn in Philadelphia remains a mystery.

The same may be said for Tom once he arrived home. Back at Monticello, he spent the next four months in seclusion. Not a single letter of his is recorded between December 10, 1775, and May 16, 1776, nor are there references to any. His Garden Book, in which he otherwise meticulously recorded every planting at Monticello, is also blank during this period, though he was home during the peak of spring planting. Apart from drawing up a list of militia volunteers from his home county—a task he had taken on as a member of Virginia's Committee of Safety—

Tom apparently did little but care for Patty during those months.

In February, Tom received a letter from his friend and fellow delegate in Philadelphia, Thomas Nelson. Peyton Randolph's widow had returned to Virginia after her husband's death, but Nelson and his wife still occupied the same living quarters they had shared with Tom above Benjamin Randolph's cabinetry shop. "You must certainly bring Mrs. Jefferson with you," Nelson urged, adding that his wife would "take all possible care of her."

Tom agonized over what to do. Duty demanded that he return to Philadelphia. But Patty was in no condition to make the seven-day trip, to say nothing of the miasmatic night air and the other health hazards to which she would be exposed in that overcrowded city. And he was not about to leave her alone.

Tom was preparing to go back by himself when another family tragedy struck. On March 31, he wrote in his account book: *"My mother died about 8 o'clock this morning, in the 57th year of her age."* She, like her cousin Peyton Randolph, had fallen victim to an apoplectic stroke, and though all of her children were grown, her death no doubt added to his mental burden.

Right after this, Tom suffered a blinding, debilitating headache. For the next six weeks it coursed from his temples through his entire head, throbbing relentlessly day and night. One might speculate on the cause. Was it his anxiety over Patty's health? The stress over his mother's unexpected death? His reluctance to leave home? Tom had planned to leave for Philadelphia at the end of March. Perhaps it was brought on by an unconscious desire to find an excuse, no matter how tortuous, to delay his departure.

The next Virginia Convention was scheduled to convene in Williamsburg on May 6. Dr. George Gilmer, Tom's friend and family physician, had been re-elected to represent Albemarle County. Tom sent a messenger to

Gilmer's home. The ostensible reason was to ask him to come and treat his headache. But the main reason was to ask him a favor.

"Please," Tom said after Gilmer put away his stethoscope, "can you find someone to replace me in Congress?"

"I'll see what I can do," Gilmer said.

Meanwhile, Thomas Paine, the London corset-maker Benjamin Franklin had talked into moving to Philadelphia, exploded into print with a pamphlet titled *Common Sense.* Condemning King George III as "the greatest enemy this continent hath," the blunt, English-born freethinker minced no words in his call for independence:

The sun never shined on a cause of greater worth. The blood of the slain, the weeping voice of nature, cries, 'TIS TIME TO PART.'

Thomas Nelson, still holding forth in Congress, sent Tom a copy from Philadelphia where the author had it published at his own expense. "I send you a present of 2/ worth of Common Sense," Nelson wrote.

Paine's message spread through the colonies like wildfire. Spurred into action, Tom sounded out his neighbors in Albemarle and nearby counties. Nine out of ten favored independence.

By early May, Tom was over his headache. He felt renewed, refreshed. It was high time he put in his appearance at Congress. He didn't know it then, but to delay any longer would mean missing his chance of joining the company of immortals.

Finally, on May 7, he took out his account book, wrote *"Left with Mrs. Jefferson £10"* to cover household expenses, and set out for Philadelphia for the last time.

CHAPTER THIRTEEN

Philadelphia – May 1776

"For God's sake, declare the colonies independent at once and save us from ruin."
—John Page to Thomas Jefferson

When Tom arrived at his post a week later, the war dispatches that greeted him from the north were both good and bad. In Boston, General Washington had driven out the British; royal navy ships were retreating to Halifax, their holds filled with wounded redcoats. But in Quebec, where the Americans had sought to capture the British base of operations, Benedict Arnold lost most of his army to disease and starvation. As for Ethan Allen, nothing had come of Tom's appeal for his release; he would remain a prisoner-of-war another two years. From Canada in the north to Virginia in the south, the once-limited revolt had grown into a full-scale armed rebellion.

In the war-of-words, Paine's *Common Sense* continued to sweep through the colonies. Its denunciations of King George III—and monarchy in general—resounded in every city, town and hamlet:

A thirst for absolute power is the natural disease of monarchy.

In England a King hath little more to do than to make war and give away places.

Of more worth is one man to society and in the sight of God than all the crowned ruffians that ever lived.

We have it in our power to begin the world over again.

When Tom checked into his lodgings on Chestnut Street, he found a letter waiting for him from John Page, his friend back in Virginia. "For God's sake," he pleaded, "declare the colonies independent at once and save us from ruin."

Page had written him from Williamsburg where the next Virginia Convention was about to meet. With Lord Dunmore out of striking distance, the delegates had moved their convention from Richmond to Williamsburg where they had retaken the capitol. In the same house chamber where many had served as burgesses in happier days, they were about to embark on their boldest mission yet: proclaiming their colony's own independence from England (forget the foot-dragging in Philadelphia!) and creating a new government for their independent commonwealth.

Had he any say in the matter, Tom would have chosen to be in Williamsburg, not Philadelphia, because that's where the action was. Besides, it was closer to home. Three days after he arrived, he wrote his fellow delegate to Congress, Thomas Nelson, who had returned to Williamsburg for the Virginia Convention:

Dear Nelson:

I arrived here last Tuesday after being detained six weeks longer of a malady of which Gilmer can inform you.

Somewhat timidly, Tom broached the subject of the convention recalling its delegates to Congress—which of course would include himself—to help write Virginia's new constitution:

Should our Convention propose to establish now a form of government, perhaps it might be agreeable to recall for a short time their delegates. It is a work of the most interesting nature and such as every individual would wish to have his voice in. In truth it is the whole object of the present controversy.

But the main reason he wrote Nelson was to confess his anxiety over Patty:

I am here in the same uneasy anxious state in which I was last fall without Mrs. Jefferson who could not come with me.

Even among the foot-draggers in Congress, Paine's *Common Sense* was taking hold. Only three months before, James Wilson of Pennsylvania, writing for a committee of Congress, declared that independence was not America's goal. "What we aim at," he wrote, "is the defense and re-establishment of the constitutional rights of the colonies." But the mood was changing. *Independence*—that once-dreaded word—was now being uttered around the country. Exulted John Adams in Philadelphia: "Every post and every day rolls in upon us Independence like a Torrent."

Congress was marking time until Virginia determined on its course. Tom Jefferson and everyone else in Congress knew the real decision would be made in Williamsburg, not in Philadelphia. On May 15—although he didn't know it yet— the Virginia Convention declared that colony's independence from England. Later that day, by unanimous vote, the convention instructed its delegates in Congress to do the same for all the colonies.

***

"For God's sake, declare the colonies independent at once."

John Page's words echoed in Tom's head. But without instructions from Williamsburg, the delegates in Philadelphia could do nothing. All they could do was wait.

Fuming over his absence from home, and with the summer's heat fast approaching, Tom decided to leave his lodgings on Chestnut Street and seek a cooler place on the city's outskirts.

He knew his landlord, Benjamin Randolph, wouldn't be happy with the news. With Peyton Randolph and Thomas Nelson and their wives already gone, the landlord-cabinetmaker whose work he admired was about to lose the last of his tenants and thus a substantial portion of his livelihood.

"I hope this makes up for your loss, at least in part," Tom said. He handed Randolph a scrap of paper.

Randolph looked at the scrap of paper. It showed a rough sketch of a box with measurements written in inches: 9 ¾ by 14 3/8 by 3 ½. It had a folding board on top and a drawer on the side.

"Can you build this for me?" Tom asked.

"I'll see what I can do," Randolph said, and they agreed on a price.

The lodgings Tom found were in a new three-story brick house on the western edge of town. It stood at the corner of Seventh and Market Streets and was owned by a bricklayer named Jacob Graff, newly married, who had built it for himself and his wife and infant son. They had just moved into the first floor and were seeking tenants for the upper two.

Tom took the second floor, which consisted of a bedroom and parlor and a stairwell between them. His servant, Robert, moved into a sleeping space above the third floor. From the purchase of fiddle strings recorded in his account book on May 23—the day he moved in—we know that he brought a violin with him, most likely the Cremona from John Randolph.

A few days later Benjamin Randolph delivered the writing box. Tom was pleased. "It claims no merit of particular beauty," he wrote of it later, "yet it displays itself sufficiently for any writing." Made of mahogany, it had a green baize-lined folding board attached to the top and a drawer for paper and pens.

Tom placed the writing box on the table and began drafting a new constitution for Virginia. Not only did he want the gentlemen in Williamsburg to get it right, but it gave him something to do. And it helped take his mind off Patty.

He rushed his draft to Edmund Pendleton, the Virginia Convention's new speaker, but alas, it arrived too late. The convention had come up with another version, and they were too worn out to start over.

That wasn't the only bad news Tom received from Williamsburg. George Gilmer, his family doctor and Albemarle County's representative to the Virginia

Convention, had promised Tom to present his case for being replaced in Congress. Unable to attend, Gilmer relegated the task to another delegate, Edmund Randolph. After the convention, Randolph informed Tom of the outcome:

Dear Sir: Gilmer, not being able to attend the Convention the other Day when the delegates were chosen, sent a memo to me, to press your non-election. I urged it in decent Terms: but stirred up a Swarm of Wasps about my Ears, who seemed suspicious, that I designed to prejudice you.

After a half-hour debate, the assembly rejected Tom's plea and elected him to another year in Philadelphia.

Except for John Adams, no delegate in Congress was more eager to get on with the business of independence than Richard Henry Lee of Virginia. Referring to his countrymen back home who had taken the lead in this endeavor, he wrote Patrick Henry, who would become the state's first elected governor: "Ages yet unborn, and millions existing at present, must rue or bless that Assembly (of Virginia), on which their happiness or misery will so eminently depend."

Finally, the Virginians' instructions arrived in Philadelphia. The die was cast. But Tom, still reeling over the rejection of his plea in Williamsburg, remained at his post, fretting daily over every courier that came without a letter from Patty.

CHAPTER FOURTEEN

Philadelphia – June 1776

"Resolved, that these colonies are and of right ought to be free and independent states...."
—Virginia's Resolution to the Continental Congress, June 7, 1776

On Friday, June 7, in the hot and muggy Assembly Room of the Pennsylvania State House, Richard Henry Lee stood at Virginia's table and read the long-awaited resolution from Williamsburg:

Resolved, that these colonies are and of right ought to be free and independent states, that they are absolved from all allegiance to the British crown, and that all connection between them and the State of Great Britain is, and ought to be, totally dissolved.

John Adams leaped to his feet and seconded the motion. If he and Lee had hoped to force an instant vote, they were sadly mistaken. The moderates moved to postpone debate until the next day. At 10 o'clock Saturday morning the delegates reassembled. The opposition, led by John Dickinson and Edward Rutledge, declared that while they were friends of the measure, they opposed independence until the voice of the people drove them to it. Furthermore, they argued, certain colonies might secede from the union if independence were declared before their voice was heard.

The threat to secede, however veiled, didn't go unnoticed. "The people wait for us to lead the way!" countered Adams. "It is vain to wait weeks or months for perfect unanimity. It is impossible that all men should ever become of one sentiment on any question."

Silently, Tom sat at his table taking notes.

The debate rumbled into the night with no end in sight. Finally, on Monday, June 10, the two sides reached a compromise: postpone the vote until July 1. That would give the middle colonies three weeks to write their assemblies for instructions and hear back. But just in case Lee's resolution passes, appoint a committee to draw up a formal declaration.

The next day, June 11, Congress elected five men to the task. Secretary Thomson duly recorded their names in the minutes: John Adams of Massachusetts, Benjamin Franklin of Pennsylvania, Roger Sherman of Connecticut, Robert Livingston of New York, and Thomas Jefferson of Virginia. To his astonishment, Tom received the most votes.

Who was to write it? Franklin was confined to a friend's home outside of town with an attack of the gout, and neither Sherman nor Livingston had any literary reputation, so the choice came down to Adams and Jefferson. Tom urged the job on his Massachusetts colleague, but Adams declined.

"Why will you not?" Tom asked. "You ought to do it."

"I will not."

"Why?"

"Reasons enough."

"What can be your reasons?"

"Reason first, you are a Virginian, and a Virginian ought to appear at the head of this business. Reason second, I am obnoxious, suspected and unpopular. You are very much otherwise. Reason third, you can write ten times better than I can."

So Tom went to work. For the next seventeen days, before and after the business hours of Congress, he labored over his writing box on the second floor of Jacob Graff's house, an inkwell at his side. His quill scratched tirelessly, carving and polishing the words. He wrote in a fine, clear, meticulous script, aware that each word counted.

That Lee's resolution for independence would pass was far from certain. Holdouts like John Dickinson of

Pennsylvania and Edward Rutledge of South Carolina still had to be persuaded. But if by some miracle Lee's resolution passed, Tom's job was to give it a philosophical foundation. As a result, the ideas he so carefully forged into words were not his alone, they were universal. Thus he began:

When in the Course of human events it becomes necessary for one people to dissolve the political bands which have connected them with another, and to assume among the powers of the earth the separate and equal station to which the Laws of Nature and Nature's God entitle them, a decent respect to the opinions of mankind requires that they should declare the causes which impel them to the separation.

He dipped his quill back into the inkwell and continued:

We hold these truths to be sacred and undeniable, that all men are created equal, that they are endowed by their creator with certain inalienable rights, that among these are life, liberty and the pursuit of happiness....

The sentiments belonged to mankind. His purpose, he said later, wasn't to find out new principles or new arguments never before thought of, but to place before mankind the common sense of the subject, in short to express the American mind.

Yet even as he wrote, he had a lurking sense that he was risking, perhaps even sacrificing his beloved Patty to the cause. On June 30, he wrote to Edmund Pendleton, the president of the Virginia Convention still meeting in Williamsburg: "I am sorry the situation of my domestic affairs renders it indispensably necessary that I should solicit the substitution of some other person here in my room. The delicacy of the house will not require me to enter minutely into the private causes which render this necessary."

Adding to his anxiety, he worried about the fallout over his attempt to be replaced in Congress. On July 1, he wrote to his friend William Fleming: "It is a painful situation to be 300 miles from one's own country and thereby open to secret assassination without a possibility of self-defense." To reassure his colleagues back home that he was still on board with independence he added: "If any doubt has arisen as to me, my country will have my political creed in the form of a declaration &c., which I was lately directed to draw."

Along with his desire to express the American mind, Tom poured deep personal anguish into the Declaration. When he finished, he journeyed by horseback to Edward Duffield's house on Bristol Pike where Franklin was recovering from the gout. Adams was seated at a table with Franklin. Tom handed his draft to the older gentleman.

"Strike *sacred and deniable*," Franklin said after reading the preamble.

"Why?" Tom asked.

"It's too dogmatic. Besides it's obvious."

"Is that the word you want—*obvious?* Adams said. "We hold these truths to be *obvious?*

"Are you familiar with Euclid's *Elements?* Franklin asked.

"I read them in school," Adams said. "But what on earth does that have to do—"

Franklin interrupted. *"Things that are equal to the same thing are equal to each other.* Euclid's first axiom. All of mathematics, he said, is based upon axioms—truths that are self-evident."

Franklin looked at Tom's draft again. *"All men are created equal.* Isn't that also self-evident? *We hold these truths to be self-evident."* He handed the paper back to Tom. "Yes, let that be our axiom." He turned to Adams. *Self-evident?"*

Adams nodded his assent. "Self-evident."

"Self-evident it is then," said Tom, reluctantly making the correction.

Franklin wasn't quite finished. "Go back to the sentence about the king abetting the slave trade to the colonies. How did you phrase that?"

Tom flipped a few pages and read from his draft:

The Christian king of Great Britain has waged cruel war against human nature in the persons of a distant people who never offended him, captivating and carrying them into slavery in another hemisphere.

"Yes, that's it," Franklin said. "You blame the slave trade on the king. In fact, that endeavor goes back to the fifteen-hundreds, long before his time, and it's one in which other countries—Spain, Portugal, the Netherlands—are equally complicit. Moreover, you say nothing of slavery itself. If the slave trade is outlawed, wouldn't the slaves already on our shores become—how shall I put it—a more lucrative commodity?"

"That wasn't my purpose," Tom said. "Slavery is an insult to human nature. Indeed, I tremble that God's justice cannot sleep forever. But the issue before us is independence, not emancipation."

Franklin paused before responding. "I concede the point," he said.

It was Adams' turn to speak. "It is good, sir," he said. "I admire the high tone and the flights of oratory. But my concern is not unlike Dr. Franklin's. In your list of charges, you call the king a tyrant. The expression is too personal, too scolding, for so grave and solemn a document."

Tom returned to his apartment. Back at his writing box, he meticulously rewrote the draft and added sixteen corrections of his own. When he was finally satisfied, he presented it to the committee for approval. "We shall see how it fares on the floor," Adams said.

On Friday, June 28, the committee presented Tom's hand-written declaration to John Hancock, the president of the Continental Congress. Hancock ordered it to "lie on the table." Congress had to vote on Lee's resolution first. Which way the vote would go was anybody's guess. Would it bring Tom's declaration to life? Or would it condemn his work to oblivion?

On July 1, a few dozen men at the Pennsylvania State House would be taking up that question. And no less than the birth of a nation was at stake.

CHAPTER FIFTEEN

Philadelphia – July 1-4, 1776

"We hold these truths to be self-evident, that all men are created equal ..."
—*Final draft of Jefferson's Declaration of Independence*

Monday, July 1, began hot and steamy. From their lodgings around the city, the delegates converged on the Pennsylvania State House at 9 o'clock in the morning. Congress started the day with routine business like any other day: the reading of letters from General Washington and his officers in the field, a report from the army's paymaster, a request from Virginia to help pay for its defenses.

But soon it became clear this day would not be like any other day, nor would the few days to follow. At noon John Hancock stepped down from the president's chair as Congress reconvened into a committee of the whole; this meant that any debate or votes would be unofficial. Benjamin Harrison, his jovial good humor oddly incongruous with the moment, took his seat as chairman of the committee of the whole. The independence and anti-independence factions formed on opposite sides of the room. On the independence side were the radicals led by the two Adams cousins—John and Samuel—and Richard Henry Lee. On the anti-independence side were the conservatives led by John Dickinson and James Wilson of Pennsylvania, Robert Livingston of New York, and Edward Rutledge of South Carolina.

Dickinson and his allies knew the odds were against them, but how the vote would go was anything but certain. New Jersey's newly elected delegates had not yet arrived, nor had voting instructions from Maryland, which Samuel Chase had promised to send. And Delaware was deadlocked with two delegates on the floor—one for, one against. Delaware's third delegate and potential tie-breaker, Caesar Rodney, was nowhere to be found.

Dickinson rose first. Lean and pale and dressed in a plum-colored coat and breeches, he clung to his chair to steady himself. "The survival of our nation is at stake," he began, his voice in a slight tremor. "To abandon the protection of Great Britain by declaring independence now would be like destroying our house in winter and exposing a growing family before we have got another shelter."

As he spoke, a doorman handed John Adams an envelope postmarked Annapolis. Adams tore it open and read: "I am this moment from the House"—a reference to the Maryland assembly—"with a unanimous vote for independence…Your friend, S. Chase."

Without saying a word about the message from Maryland, Adams rose to answer Dickinson. "This is an idle mispense of time," he scoffed, "for nothing has been said but what has been repeated and hackneyed in this room before a hundred times for six months past."

So the debate went for the next four hours. Meanwhile, the mid-summer sky turned an ominous black. A thunderstorm crept in over the State House. Adams continued to speak as rain pelted the windows and flashes of lightning lit up the assembly room. Adams was still on his feet when three rain-soaked delegates arrived from New Jersey with instructions to vote for independence.

It was late afternoon when Harrison called for an unofficial vote. Nine colonies voted *yay*; two—South Carolina and Pennsylvania—voted *nay*. Delaware, with only two delegates on the floor, was split; and New York, still awaiting instructions from their assembly, abstained. Instead of unifying the colonies, the question of independence threatened to divide and destroy them.

Congress had a choice. Either it could go back into open session and force Lee's resolution through with a two-thirds majority. Or it could delay the official vote. Forcing the vote now would mean the nay-sayers would remain under British rule—unless they had a change-of-heart later, but what would they do then?

It was Edward Rutledge of South Carolina, ironically one of the nay-sayers, who came to the rescue. "Let's postpone the vote until tomorrow," he said. Congress gratefully agreed to his motion and Harrison's gavel fell, dissolving the committee of the whole.

A night of frantic, back-room politicking followed. To break Delaware's deadlock, John Adams and his pro-independence faction conspired to send an express rider to Dover, Delaware—some seventy miles away—to summon Caesar Rodney and his pro-independence vote. John Dickinson was admonished to vote yay or stay home; it didn't help to remind him that mostly pro-independence men had just been elected to his own Pennsylvania assembly. Benjamin Franklin, still recovering from the gout, lectured Edward Rutledge and his anti-independence men on the importance of unity. "We must all hang together," he warned, "or most assuredly we will all hang separately."

The next morning, Tuesday, July 2, Congress reconvened. The previous day's thunderstorm had lowered the heat, leaving a dry, cooler day for the colonies to decide their fate. John Hancock took the president's chair. Caesar Rodney, caked in mud after riding all night through the storm, took his seat at Delaware's table.

Again, Hancock opened the session with the routine business of the day—letters from General Washington and the Council of Massachusetts Bay, an expense report from the army's paymaster general.

And again, Benjamin Harrison took the chair as Congress resolved itself into a committee of the whole. Rodney, exhausted after his all-night ride, seized the moment to speak: "As I believe the voice of my constituents and of all sensible and honest men is in favor of independence and my own judgment concurs with them, I vote for independence." Edward Rutledge declared "for the sake of unity" that he was doing the same.

The debate was done. John Dickinson left his place at Pennsylvania's table as Hancock resumed the president's chair. Charles Thomson, at the secretary's table, reread Richard Henry Lee's resolution: "That these colonies are and of right ought to be free and independent states...."

Hancock called for the vote. All the colonies but one voted *aye*. The one that didn't was New York—not because it was opposed, but because its delegates to Congress hadn't yet received their instructions. Until then, New York was an abstention.

But the deed was done. "The second day of July," John Adams declared jubilantly, "will be the most memorable epocha in the history of America...It ought to be solemnized with pomp and parade, with shows, games, sports, guns, bells, bonfires, and illuminations from one end of the continent to the other, from this time forward, forevermore."

The fact of independence was accomplished. Now it was time to take up the declaration that would justify it to the world. The next morning, July 3, Congress resolved itself into a committee of the whole and Benjamin Harrison took the chair. At once the sharp-witted lawyers fell upon Tom's creation with a zeal that cut him to the quick. For the rest of the day Congress slashed away at his paper, slicing off offensive words and phrases as if they were cancerous tissue. Congress adjourned late in the afternoon, its scalpel poised to finish the job the next day.

Unable to bear the mutilation of his precious work, Tom's thoughts turned homeward and to Patty. On his way to the State House the next morning, Thursday, July 4, he stopped at an open-air market and bought her seven pairs of women's gloves and a thermometer to hang at Monticello.

When Tom resumed his seat, so did the torture. Word by word, paragraph by paragraph, Congress continued to slash away at his paper. Edward Rutledge and others from the south insisted that his attack on the slave trade be thrown out. Let South Carolina and Georgia have their slave trade, the majority finally conceded. If America won the war, then there would be time to do something about slavery. But if the slave trade was going to be a deal-breaker, then it would be their own dirty business to deal with.

Tom agonized through the ordeal. For propriety's sake he sat still and silent while Benjamin Harrison drew his official pen through the author's precious phrases. The burden of defense fell on Adams who jumped up repeatedly, fighting fearlessly for every word, forging a debt of friendship the author never forgot.

Dr. Franklin rose from his chair, but it wasn't to address the assembly. He hobbled with his cane over to Tom whose downcast eyes were fixed on the floor.

"Tom," he said, his voice barely above a whisper, "remember what I told you about drafting public papers and why I always sought to avoid it? Well, this is why."

Tom looked up and saw a twinkle in the old man's eyes.

"John Thompson had an experience like yours," Franklin said.

"John Thompson?"

"A hatmaker here in town." Franklin took an open chair next to Tom and hooked his cane over the armrest. "Mr. Thompson made a sign for his hat shop that said, 'JOHN THOMPSON, HATTER, MAKES AND SELLS HATS FOR READY MONEY,' and it displayed a hat underneath. He showed the sign to his friends and they all hacked away at it. One of them said, "What do you mean, *sells* hats? Nobody expects you to *give* them away!"

"So?"

"Mr. Thompson's sign ended up with just his name and the hat."

Out of the more than eighteen hundred words in Tom's draft, Congress expunged four hundred and sixty, about one-fourth, including Tom's passage accusing George III of waging "cruel war against human nature" by abetting the slave trade to the colonies.

Finally, on the evening of July 4 the slashing ceased. John Hancock, back in the president's chair, called for the vote: twelve *yeas*, no *nays*, one abstention. The same as two days before on Lee's resolution for independence. New York's instructions still had not arrived. When they finally did on July 15, Hancock declared the vote unanimous.*

It wasn't until Friday, August 2, that an engrossed copy was prepared and laid out on the president's table for everyone to sign. Hancock went first, declaring he wanted George III to see his enormous signature without his spectacles. Forty-nine other delegates signed that day and six more added their names later, making a total of fifty-six.

Only a few including John Adams recognized the monumental importance of what those fifty-six gentlemen in Philadelphia had accomplished. But all knew the risk involved. Portly Benjamin Harrison, as he took up the quill, attempted a bit of gallows humor. To the slightly-built Elbridge Gerry of Massachusetts standing beside him he remarked: "I shall have a great advantage over you, Mr. Gerry, when we are all hung for what we are now doing. From the size and weight of my body I shall die in a few minutes, but from the lightness of your body, you will dance in the air an hour or two before you are dead."

President Hancock ordered a public reading of the Declaration on July 8. Hundreds of townspeople embraced and cheered in the State House yard while Col. John Nixon, a local tavern keeper, read Tom's words from the

*Hancock made the announcement after Lewis Morris, who had gone back to his assembly for instructions, returned with a *yea* vote on behalf of New York.

balcony of an observatory tower. Church bells rang into the night.

But of all the patriots celebrating the Declaration, Tom was probably the least able to enjoy it. Not only had Congress destroyed his pride of authorship, but the letters from home stopped coming again. "I wish I could be better satisfied on the point of Patty's recovery," he wrote his brother-in-law Francis Eppes on July 15. "I have not heard from her at all for two posts before, and no letter from herself now."

His anxiety wasn't helped by Virginia's thinning ranks in the Congress. Debate had turned to the Articles of Confederation, and one by one the Virginia delegates were inventing excuses to go home. Almost before he knew it, Tom was left as the sole guardian of Virginia's vote. On July 29 he issued a plea to Richard Henry Lee, who had gone home like the others but was due back any day: "For God's sake, for your country's sake, and for my sake, come."

The next day he wrote to his friend John Page, giving his take on the month in Philadelphia that changed the course of history.

"There is nothing new here," he wrote.

"I propose to leave this place by the 11th of August, having so advised Mrs. Jefferson by last post…Every letter brings me an account of the state of her health, that it is with great pain that I stay here."

The 11th of August came and left. Lee had not yet arrived. By September 3, Tom couldn't stand it any longer. Checking out of his lodgings, he wrote in his account book, *"Pd. Mrs. Graff in full 25/,"* and set out for home in his phaeton, vowing to get out of politics. At thirty-three he had had enough.

En route he stopped at The Forest to retrieve his ailing wife and now four-year-old daughter, Patsy. The next day they arrived at their beloved Monticello. The sun fell gloriously on the mountaintop, but another thunderstorm was gathering in the valley below.

EPILOGUE

Monticello – July 4, 1826

"Thomas Jefferson still survives."
—John Adams, July 4, 1826

For years Thomas Jefferson's authorship of the Declaration of Independence remained an obscure fact of history known only to a few close friends and his colleagues in the Second Continental Congress. Astonishingly, it was never publicly acknowledged until a Boston newspaper mentioned it in 1784. As late as 1800 Jefferson himself ranked it second in his own list of public accomplishments. At the top: his clearing the Rivanna River near his home for shipping tobacco.

If Jefferson's preoccupations were mostly domestic in the years after the Declaration, they continued to be dominated by his wife Patty's health. In the first six years after he returned from Philadelphia, she bore him four more children, but only two survived infancy. On May 3, 1782, the last was born. The child thrived, but the mother failed to recover. For four months Jefferson nursed her with desperate tenderness. Propped up in her bed, Patty opened the pages of *Tristam Shandy,* a popular novel of the period, and copied the following lines:

Time wastes too fast; every letter I trace tells me with what rapidity life follows my pen. The days and hours of it are flying over our heads like clouds of windy day never to return—more everything passes on—

That was as far as her strength could take her. In a clear, firm hand her husband completed the quotation:

—and every time I kiss thy hand to bid adieu, every absence which follows it are preludes to that eternal separation which we are shortly to make!

On September 6, 1782, Jefferson recorded the saddest of all the items in his incredible account book: "*My dear wife died this day at 11:45 a.m.*"

To assuage his grief, he plunged back into the political life he once vowed to avoid. During the next twenty-six years he was to serve as a United States Congressman, minister to France, Secretary of State, Vice President, and President for two terms. He never remarried. Of his six children, only Patsy survived him. Another daughter, Mary, died in 1804 at the age of twenty-five, two months after her father was renominated for President.

It's a sad irony of history that when Jefferson should have been celebrating two of the greatest events of his public life—the Declaration of Independence and his landslide re-election to the Presidency—he was privately tormented by anxiety and grief over two of the people closest to him.

Jefferson may have wondered whether his public service was worth the personal price. Had he been home during the summer of 1776 when his wife most needed him, had he not exposed her to the rigors of the Revolutionary War that later attended his term as governor of Virginia, would she have lived beyond her thirty-three years? Indeed, if she had, would Jefferson—whose fondest wish in life was to enjoy domestic tranquility at Monticello with his wife and daughters and scientific pursuits—have become President?

Whatever the answers, Jefferson's last great wish—to live to the fiftieth anniversary of the Declaration of Independence—bears testimony to the significance he and the rest of the world came to attach to that document. Two days before his death he handed Patsy a little poem that read in part:

...Farewell, my dear, my lov'd daughter adieu!
The last pang of life is in parting from you!
Two seraphs await me long shrouded in death;
I will bring them your love on my last parting breath.

Jefferson slept through the night. When he awoke he remarked, "This is the fourth of July." It was only the third.

He fought with every ounce of his ebbing energy to live to the great day. Finally, at fifty minutes past noon, on July 4, 1826, he died—fifty years to the day after the Declaration of Independence.

Five hundred miles to the north, in Quincy, Massachusetts, his old friend and compatriot in the Congress, John Adams, was also dying. Of all the delegates back in 1776, he had fought the hardest for independence. He too wanted to see the great day.

When Adams said his last words early that evening, he didn't know that his friend had died just hours before. But now they had another meaning. "Thomas Jefferson," he said, "still survives."

CHRONOLOGY

March 23, 1775—Patrick Henry gives his famous "Give me liberty, or give me death" speech at the Second Virginia Convention.

March 27, 1775—Jefferson is elected to the Second Continental Congress as a deputy (substitute) for Peyton Randolph.

March 28, 1775—Lord Dunmore, the royal governor of Virginia, forbids the appointment of delegates to the Continental Congress.

April 19, 1775—Battle at Lexington and Concord.

April 20, 1775—Lord Dunmore orders the confiscation of the colony's gunpower in Williamsburg.

May 10, 1775—Second Continental Congress convenes in Philadelphia.

May 18, 1775—Congress receives news of the capture of Fort Ticonderoga.

May 24, 1775—Congress elects John Hancock president, replacing Peyton Randolph, who has been recalled to Virginia to preside over the House of Burgesses.

June 15, 1775—Congress appoints George Washington commander of the Continental Army.

June 17, 1775—Battle at Bunker Hill.

June 20, 1775—Jefferson arrives in Philadelphia to take his seat in Congress in place of Peyton Randolph.

June 23, 1775—General Washington departs for Boston to take command of the Continental Army.

June 27-29, 1775—Jefferson drafts Congress's *Declaration on Taking Arms*.

June 30, 1775—Committee rejects Jefferson's draft, appoints John Dickinson to rewrite it.

July 6, 1775—Congress approves Dickinson's *Declaration on Taking Arms*.

July 8, 1775—Congress signs Dickinson's "Olive Branch Petition."

July 20-30, 1775—Jefferson drafts Congress's reply to Lord North's conciliatory proposition.

July 31, 1775—Congress approves Jefferson's reply to Lord North.

August 1, 1775—Congress adjourns until September 5, 1775.

August 23, 1775—King George III issues his Proclamation for Suppressing Rebellion and Sedition.

August 26, 1775—Jefferson is elected a delegate in his own right to the Continental Congress.

September 2, 1775—Jefferson's younger daughter Jane dies at seventeen months.

September 5, 1775—Congress reconvenes.

October 1, 1775—Jefferson arrives in Philadelphia, nearly a month after Congress has reconvened.

October 22, 1775—Peyton Randolph dies of an apoplectic stroke.

November 7, 1775—Lord Dunmore issues proclamation promising freedom to slaves in Virginia who fight for the British.

November 9, 1775—Congress learns of King George III's rejection of the "Olive Branch Petition."

December 2, 1775—Jefferson drafts a petition for the release of Ethan Allen, captured by the British at Montreal.

December 22, 1775—Parliament and the King approve the Prohibitory Act, effectively declaring war on the American colonies.

December 28, 1775—Jefferson returns to Monticello.

January 1776—The Continental Army suffers devastating defeats in Canada.

January 1776—Thomas Paine publishes *Common Sense*.

March 4, 1776—General Washington's army occupies Dorchester Heights in Boston; British evacuate the city.

March 31, 1776—Jefferson's mother, Jane Randolph Jefferson, dies.

May 14, 1776—Jefferson arrives back in Philadelphia to attend the Second Continental Congress.

May 15, 1776—The Virginia Convention instructs its delegates to Congress to introduce a resolution for independence.

May 1776—Jefferson begins drafting a new constitution for Virginia.

May 23, 1776—Jefferson moves to the house of Jacob Graff at Seventh and Market Streets.

June 7, 1776—Richard Henry Lee introduces the resolution for independence.

June 11, 1776—Congress appoints a committee to prepare a declaration of independence; Jefferson agrees to draft the document.

June 28, 1776—Jefferson's draft of the Declaration of Independence is submitted to Congress.

July 1, 1776—Congress begins debate on Lee's resolution for independence.

July 2, 1776—Congress adopts Lee's resolution for independence.

July 2-4, 1776—Congress debates and edits Jefferson's draft of the Declaration of Independence.

July 4, 1776—Congress adopts the Declaration of Independence.

THE DECLARATION OF INDEPENDENCE

IN CONGRESS, July 4, 1776.

The unanimous Declaration of the thirteen united States of America,

When in the Course of human events, it becomes necessary for one people to dissolve the political bands which have connected them with another, and to assume among the powers of the earth, the separate and equal station to which the Laws of Nature and of Nature's God entitle them, a decent respect to the opinions of mankind requires that they should declare the causes which impel them to the separation.

We hold these truths to be self-evident, that all men are created equal, that they are endowed by their Creator with certain unalienable Rights, that among these are Life, Liberty and the pursuit of Happiness. —That to secure these rights, Governments are instituted among Men, deriving their just powers from the consent of the governed, —That whenever any Form of Government becomes destructive of these ends, it is the Right of the People to alter or to abolish it, and to institute new Government, laying its foundation on such principles and organizing its powers in such form, as to them shall seem most likely to effect their Safety and Happiness. Prudence, indeed, will dictate that Governments long established should not be changed for light and transient causes; and accordingly all experience hath shewn, that mankind are more disposed to suffer, while evils are sufferable, than to right themselves by abolishing the forms to which they are accustomed. But when a long train of abuses and usurpations, pursuing invariably the same Object evinces a design to reduce them under absolute Despotism, it is their right, it is their duty, to throw off such Government, and to provide new Guards for their future security.–Such has been the patient sufferance of these Colonies; and such is now the necessity which constrains them to alter their former Systems of Government. The history of the present King of Great Britain is a history of repeated injuries and usurpations, all having in direct object the establishment of an absolute Tyranny over these States. To prove this, let Facts be submitted to a candid world.

He has refused his Assent to Laws, the most wholesome and necessary for the public good.

He has forbidden his Governors to pass Laws of immediate and pressing importance, unless suspended in their operation till his Assent should be obtained; and when so suspended, he has utterly neglected to attend to them.

He has refused to pass other Laws for the accommodation of large districts of people, unless those people would relinquish the right of Representation in the Legislature, a right inestimable to them and formidable to tyrants only.

He has called together legislative bodies at places unusual, uncomfortable, and distant from the depository of their public Records, for the sole purpose of fatiguing them into compliance with his measures.

He has dissolved Representative Houses repeatedly, for opposing with manly firmness his invasions on the rights of the people.

He has refused for a long time, after such dissolutions, to cause others to be elected; whereby the Legislative powers, incapable of Annihilation, have returned to the People at large for their exercise; the State remaining in the mean time exposed to all the dangers of invasion from without, and convulsions within.

He has endeavoured to prevent the population of these States; for that purpose obstructing the Laws for Naturalization of Foreigners; refusing to pass others to encourage their migrations hither, and raising the conditions of new Appropriations of Lands.

He has obstructed the Administration of Justice, by refusing his Assent to Laws for establishing Judiciary powers.

He has made Judges dependent on his Will alone, for the tenure of their offices, and the amount and payment of their salaries.

He has erected a multitude of New Offices, and sent hither swarms of Officers to harrass our people, and eat out their substance.

He has kept among us, in times of peace, Standing Armies without the Consent of our legislatures.

He has affected to render the Military independent of and superior to the Civil power.

He has combined with others to subject us to a jurisdiction foreign to our constitution, and unacknowledged by our laws; giving his Assent to their Acts of pretended Legislation:

For Quartering large bodies of armed troops among us:

For protecting them, by a mock Trial, from punishment for any Murders which they should commit on the Inhabitants of these States:

For cutting off our Trade with all parts of the world:

For imposing Taxes on us without our Consent:

For depriving us in many cases, of the benefits of Trial by Jury:

For transporting us beyond Seas to be tried for pretended offences

For abolishing the free System of English Laws in a neighbouring Province, establishing therein an Arbitrary government, and enlarging its Boundaries so as to render it at once an example and fit instrument for introducing the same absolute rule into these Colonies:

For taking away our Charters, abolishing our most valuable Laws, and altering fundamentally the Forms of our Governments:

For suspending our own Legislatures, and declaring themselves invested with power to legislate for us in all cases whatsoever.

He has abdicated Government here, by declaring us out of his Protection and waging War against us.

He has plundered our seas, ravaged our Coasts, burnt our towns, and destroyed the lives of our people.

He is at this time transporting large Armies of foreign Mercenaries to compleat the works of death, desolation and tyranny, already begun with circumstances of Cruelty & perfidy scarcely paralleled in the most barbarous ages, and totally unworthy the Head of a civilized nation.

He has constrained our fellow Citizens taken Captive on the high Seas to bear Arms against their Country, to become the executioners of their friends and Brethren, or to fall themselves by their Hands.

He has excited domestic insurrections amongst us, and has endeavoured to bring on the inhabitants of our frontiers, the merciless Indian Savages, whose known rule of warfare, is an undistinguished destruction of all ages, sexes and conditions.

In every stage of these Oppressions We have Petitioned for Redress in the most humble terms: Our repeated Petitions have been answered only by repeated injury. A Prince whose character is thus marked by every act which may define a Tyrant, is unfit to be the ruler of a free people.

Nor have We been wanting in attentions to our Brittish brethren. We have warned them from time to time of attempts by their legislature to extend an unwarrantable jurisdiction over us. We have reminded them of the circumstances of our emigration and settlement here. We have appealed to their native justice and magnanimity, and we have conjured them by the ties of our common kindred to disavow these usurpations, which, would inevitably interrupt our connections and correspondence. They too have been deaf to the voice of justice and of consanguinity. We must, therefore, acquiesce in the necessity, which denounces our Separation, and hold them, as we hold the rest of mankind, Enemies in War, in Peace Friends.

We, therefore, the Representatives of the united States of America, in General Congress, Assembled, appealing to the Supreme Judge of the world for the rectitude of our intentions, do, in the Name, and by Authority of the good People of these Colonies, solemnly publish and declare, That these United Colonies are, and of Right ought to be

Free and Independent States; that they are Absolved from all Allegiance to the British Crown, and that all political connection between them and the State of Great Britain, is and ought to be totally dissolved; and that as Free and Independent States, they have full Power to levy War, conclude Peace, contract Alliances, establish Commerce, and to do all other Acts and Things which Independent States may of right do. And for the support of this Declaration, with a firm reliance on the protection of divine Providence, we mutually pledge to each other our Lives, our Fortunes and our sacred Honor.

The 56 signatures on the Declaration:

John Hancock	*Abraham Clark*
Josiah Bartlett	*Robert Morris*
William Whipple	*Benjamin Rush*
Matthew Thornton	*Benjamin Franklin*
Samuel Adams	*John Morton*
John Adams	*George Clymer*
Robert Treat Paine	*James Smith*
Elbridge Gerry	*George Taylor*
Stephen Hopkins	*James Wilson*
William Ellery	*George Ross*
Roger Sherman	*George Read*
Samuel Huntington	*Caesar Rodney*
William Williams	*Thomas McKean*
Oliver Wolcott	*Samuel Chase*
William Floyd	*William Paca*
Philip Livingston	*Thomas Stone*
Francis Lewis	*Charles Carroll of Carrollton*
Lewis Morris	*George Wythe*
Richard Stockton	*Richard Henry Lee*
John Witherspoon	*Thomas Jefferson*
Francis Hopkinson	*Benjamin Harrison*
John Hart	*Thomas Nelson, Jr.*
Francis Lightfoot Lee	*Thomas Heyward, Jr.*

Carter Braxton
William Hooper
Joseph Hewes
John Penn
Edward Rutledge

Thomas Lynch, Jr.
Arthur Middleton
Button Gwinnett
Lyman Hall
George Walton

SOURCE NOTES

The historical facts on which this book is based are available to anyone who cares to look them up. The notes below are limited to people, places and events that figure directly in Thomas Jefferson's story.

Abbreviations of Frequently Cited Works

JAC   *Journals of the American Congress*, Vol. 1, September 5, 1774, to December 31, 1776 (Washington: Way and Gideon, 1893). Also available online at www.memory.loc.gov.

JMB   *Jefferson Memorandum Books, 1775-1776*. Available online at www.founders.archives.gov.

JTV   *Jefferson the Virginian* (Vol. 1 of *Jefferson and His Time*), Dumas Malone (Boston: Little, Brown and Co., 1949).

PTJ   *The Papers of Thomas Jefferson*, Vol. 1, 1760-1776, Julien P. Boyd, ed. (Princeton University Press, 3rd printing, 1969).

RRB   *Our Lives, Our Fortunes and Our Sacred Honor: The Forging of American Independence, 1774-1776*, Richard R. Beeman (New York: Basic Books, 2013).

Chapter One

3   *James Gunn's big yellow house: JMB.* Jefferson's account book contains several entries between March 22 and 28, 1775, which suggest he boarded there during the second Virginia convention.

3   *Mrs. Younghusband's Tavern: JMB.* Jefferson's account book entry for March 20, 1775, reads: "Pd. for punch at Mrs. Younghusband's 1/." The tavern was kept by the estranged wife of Isaac

Younghusband, a prominent Richmond merchant.

5   *Tom, whose mother was Randolph's cousin*: The Randolphs were among colonial Virginia's most prominent families. See Randolph family tree, *JTV*, 428.

5   *He had set out on horseback*: See *PTJ*, 121, for the instructions Jefferson drafted for Virginia's delegates to the First Continental Congress.

5   *"I didn't intend this to be published"*: Jefferson's instructions were published without his knowledge as *A Summary View, etc.*, first in Williamsburg, then in Philadelphia and London. *JTV*, 181.

6   *"Our emigration from England"*: The draft of Jefferson's instructions to Virginia's delegates in Congress appears in full in *PTJ*, 121-135.

7   *"I wrote it in haste"*: *JTV*, 182.

7   *Tom recognized the voice as Patrick Henry's*: The scene with Henry is imagined. Dumas Malone describes Jefferson's early association with him in *JTV*, 89-91.

8   *"I'm afraid I mislaid it"*: *JTV*, 181.

9   *"March 18, 1775. London"*: The *Virginia Gazette* can be found at www.research.colonialwilliamsburg.org.

Chapter Two

10   *Passing through the gate:* St. John's Church and the weather on that date are described by Robert Douthat Meade in *Patrick Henry: Practical Revolutionary* (New York: Lippincott, 1969), 23-24.

11   *The convention was in its fourth day:* The proceedings of the 1775 Richmond Convention are reported in the *Virginia Gazette*, April 1, 1775. www.research.colonialwilliamsburg.org.

11   *Tom looked around the sanctuary*: Descriptions of the delegates are drawn from various sources including Robert Douthat Meade's *Patrick Henry: Practical Revolutionary*, 20.

12   *"Resolved, unanimously"*: *Virginia Gazette*, April 1, 1775. www.research.colonialwilliamsburg.org. The debate on the Jamaica resolution is described in detail by William Wirt in *Sketches of the Life and Character of Patrick Henry* (Philadelphia, 1817), 133-136.

15   *"The question before this house"*: Patrick Henry's famous liberty-or-death speech, delivered extemporaneously, was pieced together by his first biographer, William Wirt, from recollections of Jefferson and others at the 1775 Virginia Convention. The full speech may be accessed at www.history.org.

16   *"Let me be buried at this spot!"*: According to Robert Douthat Meade, the observer outside the church window was Edward Carrington, a future lieutenant colonel in the Continental Army. He eventually got his wish. *Patrick Henry: Practical Revolutionary*, 36.

17   *"Resolved, that Thomas Jefferson, Esq."*: Ibid., *Virginia Gazette*, April 1, 1775. www.research.colonialwilliamsburg.org.

Chapter Three

19   *In the stable under the north terrace*: JMB. Jefferson's entry for May 7, 1775, reads: "Allycrocker's colt by young Fearnought was foaled."

19   *Was there any other place?* The description of Monticello is drawn from Jefferson's letter to Maria Cosway, October 12, 1786. founders.archives.gov/documents/Jefferson.

20   *The eyes that met his:* No life portrait of Martha
      Jefferson survives. The description of her is based
      on contemporary accounts. *JTV*, 158.

20   *"All my wishes end where I hope my days will end":*
      Jefferson to George Gilmer, August 12, 1787.
      www.founders.archives.gov/documents/Jefferson.
      Jefferson's conversation with his wife is imagined.

21   *"Patrick Henry is the laziest man for reading":* The
      Autobiography of Thomas Jefferson (New York:
      Empire Books, 2012), 15. Joseph Ellis observes
      that Jefferson's criticism of Henry's oratory
      "betrayed a certain admiration for Henry's
      capacity to sway a crowd by emotional appeals
      unencumbered with any learning or evidence."
      See *American Sphinx: The Character of Thomas
      Jefferson* (New York: Vintage Books, 1998, 44.

23   *Early that afternoon Dr. George Gilmer:* The scene
      with Dr. Gilmer is imagined. Dumas Malone
      believes that Jefferson heard the news from
      Lexington and Concord about two weeks after
      the first shots were fired. *JTV*, 197.

24   *"To all friends of American liberty": Virginia Gazette,*
      April 19, 1775.
      www.research.colonialwilliamsburg.org.

24   *"I send you three dozen bottles of Madeira":* Jefferson to
      William Small, May 7, 1775. *PTJ*, 165.

25   *Allycrocker had her colt: JMB.* Jefferson's account
      book entry for May 7, 1775, reads: "Allycroker's
      colt by young Fearnaught was foaled May 7."

27   *"The British Parliament has no right":* Virginia's
      Resolutions on Lord North's Conciliatory
      Proposal was presented June 10, 1775. The
      resolutions appear in full in *PTJ*, 170-174.

Chapter Four

28   *Except for the new red brick shops: JMB.* Jefferson
      records that he arrived in Philadelphia on June 20,
      1775. This was his first visit to Philadelphia since
      he traveled there in 1766 to be inoculated against
      smallpox.

29   *A block and a half ahead:* During his 1766 visit, and
      again in 1775, Jefferson lodged with the
      cabinetmaker Benjamin Randolph, whose house
      was on the north side of Chestnut Street between
      Third and Fourth Streets. *Ibid.*

29   *At the elegant new City Tavern:* Daniel Smith's City
      Tavern, on the west side of Second Street
      between Walnut and Chestnut, reputedly served
      more famous Americans than any other 18th
      century watering hole. *Historic Philadelphia, 320,
      322-324.*

31   *A few of the delegates were already seated:* The
      descriptions are drawn, in part, from William
      Fleming, *The Man from Monticello: An Intimate Life*
      (New York: William Morrow and Company,
      1969), 38.

32   *"Tom, this is John Adams of Massachusetts."* The
      imagined conversation between Jefferson and
      Adams is drawn from multiple sources including
      John Adams by David McCullough, *John Adams and
      the American Revolution* by Catherine Drinker
      Bowen, and *The Man from Monticello* by Thomas
      Fleming.

33   *President Hancock called on Charles Thomson:* Jefferson
      officially took his seat in Congress June 21, 1775.
      The resolution seating him also approved the
      proceedings of the Virginia Convention at
      Richmond. *JAC,* June 21, 1775.

34   *Patrick Henry took the floor and kept it most of the
      morning. JAC,* June 21, 1775.

34   *"Every delegate here considers himself an orator"*: John
      Adams to Abigail Adams, October 9, 1774.
      www.founders.archives.gov.
35   *"We are all strangers here"*: John Adams to Abigail
      Adams, June 11-17, 1775.
      www.founders.archives.gov.
35   *"America is a great, unwieldy body"*: Ibid. Quoted in
      David McCullough, *John Adams*, 88.

Chapter Five

36   *"Such is the pride and pomp of war"*: John Adams to
      Abigail Adams, June 23-27, 1775.
      www.founders.archives.gov.
37   *"He listened with visible pleasure"*: From John
      Adams's *Autobiography*, 1802-7; quoted in *John
      Adams: A Biography in His Own Words,* James
      Bishop Peabody, ed. (New York: Newsweek,
      1973), 170.
37   *"The cancer is too deeply rooted"*: John Adams to
      Moses Gill, June 10, 1775.
      www.founders.archives.gov.
38   *"We shall have nothing from them but deceit and
      hostility"*: John Adams to James Warren, July 6,
      1775. founders.archives.gov.
38   *"We're between hawk and buzzard"*: John Adams to
      James Warren, July 24, 1775.
      www.founders.archive.gov.
38   *"Resolved, that a sum not exceeding two millions"*: JAC,
      June 22, 1775.
38   *The next morning, Friday the 23rd:* Catherine Drinker
      Bowen vividly describes General Washington's
      departure for Boston in *John Adams and the
      American Revolution*, 534.
39   *"We have a bold commander"*:
      www.american.revolution.org.

39   *"Remember, Mr. Henry, what I now tell you":* George
     Washington to Patrick Henry, quoted in Ron
     Chernow: *Washington: A Life* (New York: Penguin,
     2010), 188.

40   *Lee's opinion of him had been formed:* John Adams to
     Abigail Adams, September 16, 1774.
     www.founders.archives.gov.

41   *The committee appointed to draw up the Declaration:* The
     formal title was *The Declaration on the Causes and
     Necessity of Taking Up Arms*; the delegates
     commonly referred to it as the *Declaration on
     Taking Arms. RRB,* 248.

Chapter Six

43   *It was midnight when Tom arrived:* The Massachusetts
     delegation resided at a lodging house kept by a
     Mrs. Sarah Yard on the east side of Second Street,
     across from City Tavern. David McCullough, *John
     Adams* (New York: Simon & Schuster, 2001), 83.

44   *"Apparently there are some people in New York":* John
     Adams to Abigail Adams. Paraphrased from a
     letter quoted in Catherine Drinker Bowen, *John
     Adams and the American Revolution* (New York:
     Grosset & Dunlap, 1950), 538.

44   *"Burn Boston, and make John Hancock a beggar":*
     Quoted in "John Hancock and the Bombarding
     of Boston," *Boston 1775.*

45   *"As our enemies have found we can flight like men":*
     Jefferson to George Gilmer, *PTJ,* 185.

46   *"To Francis Eppes, Esquire": PTJ,* 174.

46   *"Ninety-seven pages I wrote him":* Franklin's letter to
     his son William is lost but is described in *Benjamin
     Franklin: A Biography in His Own Words,* Thomas
     Fleming, ed. (New York: Harper & Row, 1972),
     263.

47   *The agreement decreed that if Tom died first:* The
     agreement between Jefferson and John Randolph
     filed April 12, 1771, in General Court appears in
     full in *PTJ*, 66.
48   "Mr. Dickinson was appointed too": Jefferson
     and Dickinson were officially added to the
     committee June 26, 1775. *JAC,* same date.

Chapter Seven

49   *Tom addressed the older delegate:* Thomas Fleming, *The
     Man from Monticello: An Intimate Life of Thomas
     Jefferson* (New York: William Morrow and
     Company, 1969), 40.
50   *That evening, on Monday, the 26th:* JMB. Jefferson
     records a June 26, 1775 "coach hire to
     Dickinson's." John Dickinson lived two miles
     north of Philadelphia, at a place called Fair Hills
     on Germantown Road.
50   *"I understand, sir":* Thomas Fleming, Ibid., 40
51   *"They have undertaken":* Jefferson's draft and fair
     copy of the declaration appear with an editorial
     note by Julien Boyd in PTJ, 187-203
53   *"Too much fault -finding and declamation":* William
     Livingston quoted in *JTV*, 205.
55   *"Johnny, you will be hanged":* Dickinson quoted in
     John Adams: A Biography in His Own Words, James
     Bishop Peabody, ed. (New York: Newsweek,
     1973), 173.

Chapter Eight

89   *So when he showed up:* JMB, July 1775. Jefferson
     kept a running account of his expenses at Smith's
     City Tavern. Saturday night, July 1, is assumed, as
     delegates to Congress frequently gathered there at
     the end of each week's business.

90   *"When the Lord closes a door"*: The saying comes down to us through the Rogers and Hammerstein musical, "The Sound of Music," but its origin is uncertain. The author ascribes it to Franklin based on his expressed religious views. See Walter Isaacson, *Benjamin Franklin: An American Life* (New York: Simon & Schuster, 2003), 451, and Ron Chernow, *Alexander Hamilton* Penguin Books, 2005), 35.

91   *"We're on the same committee"*: JAC. The committee, which eventually included Jefferson, wasn't formally appointed until July 22, 1775.

91   *"I have made it a rule"*: Franklin to Jefferson. Quoted by Walter Isaacson in *Benjamin Franklin: An American Life* (New York: Simon & Schuster, 2003), 310.

92   *"Our cause is just"*: JAC. John Dickinson's approved version of the *Declaration on Taking Arms* appears in full in the minutes for Thursday, July 6, 1775.

92   *"Most gracious sovereign"*: JAC. Congress's Olive Branch Petition, which Dickinson wrote, appears in full in the minutes for Saturday, July 8, 1775.

92   *"Give me the reason"*: Slightly different versions of the confrontation between Adams and Dickinson appear in *John Adams and the American Revolution* by Catherine Drinker Bowen (New York: Crosset & Dunlap, 1976), 526, and *John Adams* by David McCullough (New York: Simon & Schuster, 2001), 95. The author places Jefferson at the open window so he can eavesdrop on the confrontation.

94   *"The continued sitting of Congress"*: The letter to Peyton Randolph, president of the Virginia Convention, appears in full in *PTJ*, 223.

94   *"Ordered...that the above be sent undercover"*: JAC, Minutes of July 8, 1775.

95   *"Resolved, that the colonies of America"*: See PTJ, 225-233, for Jefferson's draft resolutions and discussion.

95   *"We are of the opinion"*: *PTJ* (footnote), 230.

95   *Monday, July 1, 1775: JAC.* Franklin's resolution was incorporated into the resolution passed on that date.

Chapter Nine

97   *"Brothers, Sachems, Warriors"*: *JAC,* July 13, 1775.

97   *"It's high time there was an end to it"*: Benjamin Harrison to George Washington, July 21, 1775. www.founders.archives.gov.

98   *Checking out of his apartment: JBM.* Jefferson's account book includes these entries for August 1, 1775: "Pd. Hiltzheimer for keeping horses &c. L9"; "Pd. ferrge over Schuylkill 1/3;" "Recd. Of Colo Harrison to form common stock of our travelling expenses L6-16."

98   *"A certain great fortune and piddling genius"*: John Adams to James Warren, July 24, 1775. www.founders.archives.gov.

99   *The trip to Richmond would take six days: JBM.* Jefferson's account book entry for August 6, 1775, reads: "Pd. breakfast &c. at Bowling Green 5/ which ends our common expenses travelling." Jefferson and Harrison pooled their expenses for the trip.

100   *"There is but one word in the paper"*: Jefferson to Samuel Harrison Smith, July 1, 1804. www.founders.archives.gov.

101   *Tom's mentor approached him in front of the church*: The scene with Jefferson and George Wythe is imagined but is based on an actual agreement Jefferson and John Randolph made April 11, 1771. See *PTJ*, 66. Also see *JBM*, August 17, 1775.

According to Jefferson's account book, he paid £13 for the violin, which dissolved the agreement on that date.

101   *"Tom, I have some other bad news"*: Again, the scene with George Wythe is imagined. William Small, who had returned to England in 1764, died February 18, 1775. It is not known when or how Jefferson received word of his death. *PTJ*, 166

102   *"I hope the returning wisdom"*: Jefferson's letter to John Randolph, dated August 25, 1775, appears in full in *PTJ*, 240.

103   *John Tazwell, the clerk, announced the result: JTV*, 209.

Chapter Ten

104   *Tom's father, one of Albemarle County's most prosperous tobacco farmers:* See Peter Jefferson/Jane Randolph family tree, *JTV*, 430.

104   *Tom's sister Martha: JTV*, 431.

104   *Tom carved out a clearing:* John Dos Passos, *Thomas Jefferson: The Making of a President* (Boston: Houghton Mifflin, 1964), 81.

104   *Some years earlier, in 1765:* Sarah N. Randolph, *The Domestic Life of Thomas Jefferson* (Monticello: Thomas Jefferson Memorial Foundation, 1967), 22. Jane Jefferson's age at death is incorrectly given as twenty-eight. The Jefferson/Randolph family tree, JTV, 430, gives her birth date as June 27, 1740, and death date as Oct. 1, 1765, which would make her twenty-five.

104   *When Tom and Patty Jefferson's second daughter, Jane, was born:* See Thomas Jefferson/Martha Wayles family tree, *JTV*, 434.

105   *It was in that cottage:* The honeymoon description is based on an account by Jefferson's great-granddaughter, who took it from a manuscript by Jefferson's daughter, Martha Randolph. See Sarah

N. Randolph, *The Domestic Life of Thomas Jefferson,* 25.

106 *Tom had designed his home:* Jack McLaughlin, *Jefferson and Monticello: The Biography of a Builder* (New York: Henry Holt and Company, 1988), 69.

106 *"It may well have been":* No stone survives to indicate where the infant Jane Randolph Jefferson's grave might be. See Robert H. Kean, "History of the Graveyard at Monticello," *The Collected Papers of the Monticello Association,* Vol.1, 1965.

106 *Tom's new Cremona violin:* Thomas Fleming, *The Man from Monticello* (New York: William Morrow and Company, 1969), 44.

106 *"I have since seen a pianoforte":* Thomas Jefferson to Thomas Adams, June 1, 1771. www.founders.archives.gov.

107 *"My days have been so wonderous free":* The song is generally considered the first secular song composed by a native-born American. www.philadelphiaencyclopedia.org.

107 *"Though we may politically differ in sentiments":* John Randolph to Jefferson, August 31, 1775. *PTJ,* 244.

108 *"Cousin Peyton is taking his wife":* Fawn M. Brodie, *Thomas Jefferson: An Intimate History* (New York: W.W. Norton and Company, 1974), 109.

108 *"Set out from Monticello for Philadelphia":* *JMB,* Sept. 25, 1775.

Chapter Eleven

109 *Over dinner at the City Tavern:* The fallout from the capture of Adams' letter is described by Catherine Drinker Bowen in *John Adams and the American Revolution* (New York: Grosset & Dunlap, 1976), 540, and by David McCullough in *John Adams* (New York: Simon & Schuster, 2001), 95.

109   *"Think of it as a happy accident"*: The exchange between Jefferson and Harrison is imagined, based on the above accounts of the captured letter. Bowen, 540, and McCullough, 95.

110   *"Don't forget we have a constitution to form"*: Paraphrased from a letter John Adams sent his wife Abigail, July 24, 1775. Quoted in Bowen, 538.

110   *Back at his Chestnut Street Lodgings: JTV*, 211.

111   *He collapsed onto the floor:* The account of Peyton Randolph's death is drawn from multiple sources including Jefferson's account book entry and footnote for October 22, 1775, *JMB*. Also see *JTV*, 211, and *RRB*, 281.

112   *"I have set apart nearly one day in every week"*: Jefferson to John Page, October 31, 1775. *PTJ*, 250.

112   *"I have never received a scrip of a pen"*: Jefferson to Francis Eppes, November 7, 1775. *PTJ*, 252.

112   *He urged Patty to remove to a place of refuge:* The letter is lost but is referred to in Jefferson's letter to Francis Eppes, November 21, 1775. *PTJ*, 264.

112   *"A Proclamation by the King"*: JAC, November 9, 1775. The full Proclamation may be found at www.history.com. It should be noted that Congress never formally declared war on England, nor England on America. Congress's Declaration on Arming and the King's Proclamation for Suppressing Rebellion were the closest approximations to formal war declarations.

113   *"I am to give you the melancholy news"*: Jefferson to John Randolph, November 29, 1775. *PTJ*, 268.

114   *Tom drafted a declaration for Allen's release: PTJ*, 276.

114   *"Dec. 28 – Pd. ferriage over Schuylkill ¼"*: Other JMB entries for that date include payments to a barber, a saddler, a blacksmith (presumably for new

horseshoes), and to Jacob Hiltzheimer for quartering Jefferson's horses.

Chapter Twelve

115   *His emancipation proclamation:* Dumas Malone makes the not-so-fine distinction between Dunmore's proclamation and Lincoln's in *JTV*, 215.

115   *Back at Monticello:* Jefferson's activities during this time are described by Dumas Malone in JTV, 215; Thomas Fleming in *The Man from Monticello* (New York: William Morrow and Company, 1969), 47, and Nathan Schachner in *Thomas Jefferson: A Biography* (New York: Thomas Yoseloff, 1969), 116.

116   *In February, Tom received a letter:* Thomas Nelson, Jr. to Thomas Jefferson, February 4, 1776, PTJ, 285.

116   *"My mother died about 8 o'clock this morning":* JMB, March 31, 1776.

116   *For the next six weeks:* Most biographers link Jefferson's headache to his mother's death, but Thomas Fleming suggests it was brought on by an unconscious desire to delay his departure for Philadelphia. See *The Man from Monticello*, 47.

116   *Dr. George Gilmer:* According to Nathan Schachner (*Thomas Jefferson: A Biography*, 116), Gilmer treated Jefferson for his headache. Jefferson's request that Gilmer find a replacement for him in Congress was probably made at that time.

117   *"I send you a present of 2/ worth of Common Sense":* Thomas Nelson, Jr. to Thomas Jefferson, February 4, 1776, *PTJ*, 286.

117   *Nine out of ten favored independence:* JTV, 217.

117   *"Left with Mrs. Jefferson £10":* JMB, May 7, 1776.

Chapter Thirteen

118   *Nothing had come of Tom's appeal:* JTV, 213.

128   *"For God's sake":* John Page to Jefferson, April 6,
       1776. *PTJ,* 287. Page apparently was unaware that
       Jefferson was at Monticello.

119   *"I arrived here last Tuesday":* Jefferson to Thomas
       Nelson, May 16, 1776. *PTJ,* 292.

119   *Only three months before:* James Wilson, under
       pressure from other delegates, later withdrew his
       address. *RRB,* 302.

120   *"Every post and every day":* Adams quoted in Nathan
       Schachner's *Thomas Jefferson: A Biography,* 117.

120   *On May 15…the Virginia Convention declared:* See
       Resolutions of the Virginia Convention Calling
       for Independence, *PTJ,* 290.

120   *"I hope this makes up for your loss":* The exchange
       between Jefferson and Benjamin Randolph is
       imagined. It isn't known precisely when Jefferson
       commissioned the writing box. See "Mr.
       Jefferson's Writing Box" by Lawrence M. Small,
       Smithsonian Magazine, February 2001.

121   *The lodgings Tom found:* The original address of the
       Graff House was 230 High Street, later
       renumbered 700 Market Street. A reconstruction
       stands at the southwest corner of Seventh and
       Market Streets. The description is pieced together
       from multiple sources including Nathan
       Schachner's *Thomas Jefferson: A Biography,* 118.

121   *"It claims no merit of particular beauty":* Jefferson to
       his granddaughter Ellen Randolph to whom he
       had given his writing box as a wedding present,
       November 1825. *Ibid.,* Lawrence M. Small,
       Smithsonian Magazine, February 2001.

121   *He rushed his draft to Edmund Pendleton:* Conflicting
       reasons are given as to why Jefferson's draft
       constitution was rejected. Thomas Fleming claims

it was too radical for the Virginia Convention (*The Man from Monticello*, 50.) Fawn Brodie says it arrived too late (*Thomas Jefferson: An Intimate History*, 117.) The author chooses the latter explanation.

122 *"Gilmer, not being able to attend the Convention"*: Edmund Randolph to Jefferson, June 23, 1776. *PTJ*, 407.

122 *"Ages yet unborn"*: Richard Henry Lee to Patrick Henry, April 20, 1776. Quoted in Nathan Schachner, *Thomas Jefferson: A Biography, 116.*

Chapter Fourteen

123 *On Friday, June 7*: The Resolution for Independence was written and introduced by R. H. Lee and seconded by John Adams. The resolution also contained provisions for forming foreign alliances and preparing a plan of confederation. *PTJ*, 298.

123 *The moderates moved to postpone debate:* Jefferson took detailed notes of the debates which Julien Boyd considers "perhaps the best single source of information" concerning the movement toward independence. See *PTJ*, 299-329.

124 *Postpone the vote until July 1: JAC,* June 10, 1776.

124 *The next day, June 11: JAC,* June 11, 1776.

124 *"Why will you not?"*: This is John Adams' recollection of the conversation many years later. Jefferson's recollection is somewhat different. Fawn Brodie, *Thomas Jefferson: An Intimate History*, 120.

125 *"When in the course of human events"*: For Jefferson's various drafts of the Declaration of Independence including the adopted version, see *PTJ*, 413-433.

125 *His purpose wasn't to find out new principles*: Jefferson to Henry Lee, May 8, 1825; quoted in *JTV*, 220.

125 *"I am sorry the situation of my domestic affairs"*: Jefferson to Edmund Pendleton, June 30, 1776. *PTJ*, 408.

126 *"It is a painful situation"*: Jefferson to William Fleming, July 1, 1776. *PTJ*, 411.

126 *He journeyed by horseback:* J.L.G. Ferris's famous painting, "Drafting the Declaration of Independence," depicts Franklin and Adams going over the text with Jefferson in his Market Street apartment. However, it's more likely the meeting took place at Edward Duffield's house on Bristol Pike. See *JTV*, 220 (footnote).

126 *"We hold these truths to be self-evident"*: Most historians believe the phrase "sacred and undeniable" was changed to "self-evident" at Franklin's suggestion. See PTJ, 413. The conversation between Franklin, Adams, and Jefferson is imagined but based on historical fact.

127 *"I tremble that God's justice cannot sleep forever"*: Inscribed at the Jefferson Memorial, the complete quotation reads as follows: "Indeed, I tremble for my country that God is just, and that his justice cannot sleep forever." Thomas Jefferson, *Notes on the State of Virginia, Query XVIII.* Reprinted in *The Life and Selected Writings of Thomas Jefferson,* Adrienne Koch and William Peden, eds. (New York: Random House, 1944), 279.

127 *"I admire the high tone and flights of oratory"*: John Adams to Timothy Pickering, August 6, 1822. *The Works of John Adams*, Vol. 2, Charles Francis Adams, ed. (New York: Library of America, 1984), 1500.

127 *On Friday, June 28: JAC,* June 28, 1776. The scene is depicted in John Trumbull's famous painting of 1817, suggesting how important the Declaration of Independence became later.

Chapter Fifteen

129   *Congress started the day:* JAC, July 1, 1776.

130   *"The survival of our nation is at stake":* No one transcribed Dickinson's speech, but his notes survive. David McCullough, *John Adams,* 126.

130   *"This is an idle mispense of time":* Same with Adams. What survives of his speech is based on his own recollections years later. Ibid., 127.

132   *Hancock called for the vote:* JAC, July 2, 1776.

132   *"The second day of July":* John Adams to Abigail Adams, July 2, 1776. Quoted in McCullough, 130.

132   *On his way to the State House:* Jefferson's purchases are recorded in JMB, July 4, 1776.

133   *The burden of defense fell on Adams:* As Jefferson put it, Adams "fought fearlessly for every word." "He (Adams) was the pillar of its support on the floor of Congress." McCullough, 135.

133   *"John Thompson, Hatter:"* Ibid., 131.

134   *Of the more than eighteen hundred words:* PTJ, 414.

134   *Finally on the evening of July 4:* JAC, July 4, 1776.

134   *Hancock declared the vote unanimous:* JAC, July 15, 1776.

134   *An engrossed copy was prepared and laid out:* The official signing took place August 2, 1776. RRB, 416.

134   *"I shall have a great advantage over you":* Fawn Brodie, *Thomas Jefferson: An Intimate History,* 124.

135   *President Hancock ordered a public reading:* RRB, 125.

135   *But of all the patriots celebrating the Declaration:* As the result of Congress's editing, Jefferson "maintained a wounded sense of betrayal by the Congress throughout the remainder of his life: Joseph L. Ellis, *American Sphinx: The Character of Thomas Jefferson* (New York: Vintage Books, 1998), 71.

135   *"I wish I could be better satisfied":* Jefferson to Francis Eppes, July 15, 1776. *PTJ,* 458.

135   *"For God's sake":* Jefferson to Richard Henry Lee, July 29, 1776. *PTJ,* 477.

135   *"There is nothing new here":* Jefferson to John Page, July 30, 1776. *PTJ,* 482.

135   *"Pd. Mrs. Graff": JMB,* September 3, 1776.

BIBLIOGRAPHY

Primary Sources:

Jefferson Memorandum Books, Thomas Jefferson's account
book entries from January 2, 1775, to December
31, 1776. Available online at
www.founders.archives.gov.
Journals of the American Congress, Vol. 1, September 5, 1774,
to December 31, 1776, inclusive (Washington:
Way and Gideon, 1893). Available online at
www.memory.loc.gov
The Papers of Thomas Jefferson, Vol. 1, 1760-1776, Julian P.
Boyd, ed. (Princeton: Princeton University Press,
3rd printing, 1969).*
The Proceedings of the (Virginia) Convention of Delegates (1774-
1776). Available online at
www.lawlibrary.wm.edu/wythepedia/library.
The Virginia Gazette, March 18, 1775 to June 30,1776.
Available online at
www.research.colonialwilliamsburg.org.

*Other Correspondence:

John Adams to Abigail Adams, Sept. 1774; Oct. 9, 1774;
June 23, 1775.
John Adams to Moses Gill, June 10, 1775.
John Adams to James Warren, July 6, 1775; July 24, 1775.
Thomas Jefferson to Maria Cosway, Oct. 12, 1786.
Thomas Jefferson to George Gilmer, Aug. 12, 1787.
Thomas Jefferson to Samuel Harrison Smith, July 1, 1804.
(All available online at
www.founders.archives.gov/documents.)

Books, Articles, Journals:

Adams, Charles Francis, ed., *The Works of John Adams*, Vol. 2 (New York: Library of America, 1984).

Allison, John Murray, *Adams and Jefferson: The Story of a Friendship* (Norman: University of Oklahoma Press, 1968).

Barker, Bill, *Becoming Jefferson: My Life as a Founding Father* (Colonial Williamsburg Foundation, 2019).

Bear, James A., Jr., ed., *Jefferson at Monticello* (Charlottesville: University Press of Virginia, 1967).

Becker, Carl, *A Study in the History of Political Ideas* (New York: Vintage Books, 1942).

Beeman, Richard R., *Our Lives, Our Fortunes, & Our Sacred Honor: The Forging of American Independence* (New York, Basic Books, 2013).

Binger, Carl, *Thomas Jefferson: A Well-Tempered Mind* (New York: W.W. Norton & Company, 1970).

Bowen, Catherine Drinker, *John Adams and the American Revolution* (New York: Grosset & Dunlap, 1976).

Brodie, Fawn, *Thomas Jefferson: An Intimate History* (New York: W.W. Norton & Company, 1974).

Chernow, Ron, *Washington: A Life* (New York: Penguin, 2010).

Chinard, Gilbert, *Thomas Jefferson: The Apostle of Americanism* (Ann Arbor: The University of Michigan Press, 1966).

Dos Passos, John, *Thomas Jefferson: The Making of a President* (Boston: Houghton Mifflin Company, 1964).

Dunaway, W.F., "The Virginia Conventions of the Revolution" (*The Virginia Law Register*, November, 1904).

Ellis, Joseph J., *His Excellency: George Washington* (Alfred A. Knopf, 2006.

Ellis, Joseph J., *American Dialogue: The Founders and Us* (New York: Alfred A. Knopf, 2018).

Ellis, Joseph J., *American Sphinx: The Character of Thomas Jefferson* (New York: Vintage Books, 1998).

Fleming, Thomas, *Benjamin Franklin: A Biography in His Own Words* (New York: Harper & Row, 1972).

Fleming, Thomas, *The Man from Monticello: An Intimate Life of Thomas Jefferson* (New York: William Morrow and Company, 1969).

Isaacson, Walter, *Benjamin Franklin: An American Life* (New York: Simon & Schuster, 2003).

Kean, Robert H, "History of the Graveyard at Monticello," *The Collected Papers of the Monticello Association*, Vol. 1, 1965.

Koch, Adrienne, and Peden, William, eds., *The Life and Selected Writings of Thomas Jefferson* (New York: Random House, 1944).

Kostyal, K.M., *Founding Fathers: The Fight for Freedom and the Birth of American Democracy* (Washington: National Geographic).

Malone, Dumas, *Jefferson the Virginian*, Vol.1 of *Jefferson and His Time* (Boston: Little, Brown and Company, 1948).

Malone, Dumas, *The Story of the Declaration of Independence* (New York: Oxford University Press, 1954).

Mayo, Bernard, *Jefferson Himself* (Charlottesville: University Press of Virginia, 1972).

McCullough, David, *John Adams* (New York: Simon & Schuster, 2001).

McLaughlin, Jack, *Jefferson and Monticello: The Biography of a Builder* (New York: Henry Holt and Company, 1990).

Meade, Robert Douthat, *Patrick Henry: Practical Revolutionary* (New York: Lippincott, 1969).

Nichols, Frederick D. and Bear, James A. Jr., *Monticello: A Guidebook* (Monticello: Thomas Jefferson Memorial Foundation, 1967).

Nieuwsma, Milton J., *Inventing America: Conversations with the Founders* (New York: Brick Tower Press, 2020).

Padover, Saul K., *Jefferson: A Great American's Life and Ideas* (New York: New American Library, 1970).

Peabody, James Bishop, ed., *John Adams: A Biography in His Own Words* (New York: Newsweek, 1973).

Peterson, Merrill D., *The Jefferson Image in the American Mind* (New York: Oxford University Press, 1962).

Peterson, Merrill D., *Thomas Jefferson and the New Nation: A Biography* (New York: Oxford University Press, 1970).

Peterson, Merrill D., ed., *Thomas Jefferson: A Profile* (New York: Hill and Wang, 1967.)

Randolph, Sarah N., *The Domestic Life of Thomas Jefferson* (Monticello—Charlottesville, VA: Thomas Jefferson Memorial Foundation, 1967).

Schachner, Nathan, *Thomas Jefferson: A Biography* (New York: Thomas Yoseloff, 1969).

Small, Lawrence M., "Mr. Jefferson's Writing Box," *Smithsonian Magazine*, February 2001.

Vidal, Gore, *Inventing a Nation: Washington, Adams, Jefferson* (New Haven: Yale University Press, 2003).

Wirt, William, *Sketches in the Life and Character of Patrick Henry* (Philadelphia, 1817).

Wood, Gordon S., *The Americanization of Benjamin Franklin* (New York: Penguin Books, 2004).

A CONVERSATION WITH THE AUTHOR

Milton Nieuwsma explains why he wrote Miracle on Chestnut Street *and reflects on Thomas Jefferson, the man and his legacy:*

So why did you write this book?

For a couple of reasons. One was to tell the story of the Declaration of Independence from Jefferson's point of view and in real time. The other reason was to restore his rightful place in history.

Why do you say that?

Well, he's had a pretty rough go of it the past few decades, first because of DNA and then because of the 1619 Project.

Can you elaborate?

Back when Jefferson was president—we're talking early 1800s—there were accusations he fathered a child by Sally Hemings, one of his slaves. It started when a muckraking journalist named James Callender spread rumors after Jefferson denied him a presidential appointment.

Was he acting out of revenge?

Absolutely, but there was no way to prove it. The rumors persisted for years. Then in 1974 Fawn Brodie, a history professor at U.C.L.A., wrote a book called *Thomas Jefferson: An Intimate History*. She contended that Jefferson fathered as many as seven children by Hemings over an eighteen-year period.

What did she base that on?

The fact that Jefferson, who was away from home a lot, was at Monticello nine months before each of the children was born. He also recorded purchases in his account book that appeared to be related. The evidence was circumstantial but pretty strong. Ironically, it was Dumas Malone whose own research revealed that Jefferson was home when Sally's children were conceived who most forcefully disputed Brodie's claim.

Who was Dumas Malone?

He was one of the preeminent Jefferson scholars of his time, along with Merrill Peterson and Julian Boyd. He had just published the fifth volume of a six-volume biography of Jefferson—this was around the same time the Brodie book came out—and I was just beginning my own research on Jefferson. I remember visiting him at the Alderman Library at the University of Virginia. When I raised Brodie's claim, he nearly threw me out of his office. He couldn't bear anyone suggesting that Jefferson would have an affair with a slave. But in the late 1990s, DNA testing proved that Jefferson fathered at least one of Sally Hemings' children.

What about the other children?

It's presumed they were fathered by Jefferson too, but it hasn't been proven. I do think Jefferson had deep feelings for her. He promised his wife before she died that he wouldn't remarry. So, did he fall in love with Sally? I think he did and she with him. But for them to get married in 18th century Virginia would have been unthinkable. Also, he had the promise to his late wife to keep.

What was the 1619 Project?

It was a journalism project the *New York Times* started on the 400th anniversary of the first slave-landing in British America. It consisted of a series of essays that contended among other things that the American Revolution was fought to preserve slavery.

Do you believe it was?

No, that's nonsense. But that's not to say slavery wasn't part of our history. It was a big part, but only a part. The problem with the 1619 Project is that it sees our whole history through that prism. Our story is a lot more complicated than that.

How do you reconcile the man who wrote "all men are created equal" with the man who owned two hundred slaves?

I don't. But lest we judge him too harshly, remember he was a product of his time and place. He lived in a slave-owning society. But he also said this about slavery: "I tremble for my country that God is just, that his justice cannot sleep forever." He made several attempts in his public life to end slavery, which is quite remarkable when you consider he was a slave-owner himself. But he always ran into resistance. It finally took the Civil War to end it.

After all your research, how well did you come to know Jefferson as a person?

That's an excellent question. There's a ton of information about him out there, but he's very difficult to comprehend. He's an enigma. Even Dumas Malone had that problem and he studied him for decades. When I wrote *Chestnut Street,* I let my imagination roll with the facts. I think that helped me understand him a little more. But he was probably an easier study as a young man in 1776 than he would have been, say, in 1800 when he ran for president. We all get more complicated as we get older. But the main thing to remember is that he was a human being, not a saint.

Can't you say that about all our Founding Fathers?

Of course. For too long we viewed them as marbled saints when in fact they were ordinary people. They had all the faults and weaknesses as the rest of us. Over the past twenty years or so, biographers have consciously humanized our Founding Fathers, including Jefferson. I think that's a good thing. It makes them more authentic.

What do you think is Jefferson's biggest legacy?

More than anyone, he defined the idea of America, the idea that individual freedom is basic to our way of life. He was our country's first human rights champion. Even with all of our problems today, our country is still a beacon of hope and freedom to people around the world. We owe that mainly to Jefferson.

This conversation is drawn in part from an interview the author gave his hometown newspaper, the Holland (Mich.) Sentinel, before the publication of this book. The article may be accessed at www.hollandsentinel.com/article/20110704/News/307049973.

ACKNOWLEDGMENTS

I wish to thank the late James A. Bear, Jr. and his staff at the Thomas Jefferson Foundation in Charlottesville, Virginia, for allowing me access to Jefferson's home at Monticello and records pertaining to his personal life. I also wish to thank the wonderful people who helped me with research at Colonial Williamsburg, the Alderman Library at the University of Virginia, and Independence National Historical Park in Philadelphia. In particular I wish to thank David Dutcher and Charles Dorman who shared many anecdotes with me about the Second Continental Congress, and Merrill D. Peterson, the distinguished Jefferson biographer, who read the first seven chapters in draft and gave his blessing to this book. Finally, I wish to thank my publisher, John Colby, for bringing Jefferson's story to the printed page, and Mike Slizewski, who designed the book. Most of all I thank my dear wife, Marilee, for her support and encouragement throughout the research and writing of this book.

ABOUT THE AUTHOR

MILTON NIEUWSMA is a two-time Emmy Award–winning writer, journalist and creator of the acclaimed PBS series *Inventing America*. For many years he traveled around the world covering stories for the *Chicago Tribune*, *Los Angeles Times*, and other major newspapers. He is the author or co-author of six books including *Kinderlager*, named "Best Book for Teens" in 2000 by the New York Public Library. His alma mater, Hope College in Holland, Michigan, honored him with a Distinguished Alumni Award in 2009. He and his wife Marilee have three children and seven grandchildren.

CPSIA information can be obtained
at www.ICGtesting.com
Printed in the USA
BVHW010528010722
641072BV00006B/77/J

9 781899 694952